POCKET GUIDES

TO THE PRIMARY CURRICULUM

Life processes and living things

Neil Burton

Provides the knowledge you need
to teach the primary curriculum

Author
Neil Burton

Editor
Joel Lane

Assistant Editor
David Sandford

Cover design
Joy Monkhouse
Rachel Warner

Designer
Micky Pledge

Illustrations
Garry Davies
Sally Alexander

Cover photograph
Calvin Hewitt

Published by Scholastic Ltd,
Villiers House,
Clarendon Avenue,
Leamington Spa,
Warwickshire CV32 5PR

Text © 2001 Neil Burton
© 2001 Scholastic Ltd

1234567890 1234567890

British Library Cataloguing-in-Publication
Data
A catalogue record for this book is
available from the British Library.

ISBN 0-590-53896-9

Every effort has been made to ensure that
websites and addresses referred to in this
book are correct and educationally sound.
They are believed to be current at the
time of publication. The publishers
cannot be held responsible for subsequent
changes in the address of a website, nor
for the content of the sites mentioned.
Referral to a website is not an
endorsement by the publisher of that site.

CONTENTS

Life processes

INTRODUCTION

What is a primary scientist?

There is an important distinction to be made between
scientists and primary science teachers. A scientist follows a
particular strand of science as far as possible in order to
explain it. A primary science teacher tries to understand the
scientific links between things around him or her, and to
help others achieve a better understanding of them. A good
primary science teacher is interested in helping children to
understand ideas, explain them and link them together. The
words 'explore', 'investigate' and 'Why do you think that
happened?' are much more likely to come from such a
teacher than 'Learn this by heart' or 'You don't need to
understand it, just remember it!'

How can this book help?

Having taught primary science within primary schools,
initial teacher education and continuing professional
development over the last fifteen years, I am convinced that
there has been a steady improvement in the level of
teachers' background science knowledge. I am less
convinced that this has been entirely transferred to an
understanding of the concepts at a level at which teachers
are secure and confident. To have a level of understanding
that allows you to pass on 'facts' with a fair degree of
accuracy is not enough. You need to have a 'feel' for the
subject that will allow you to appreciate where the children
are 'coming from' and enable you to help them learn more
effectively.

    This book attempts to avoid a 'GCSE science – revisited' approach. GCSE textbooks serve a particular purpose well: to get pupils through a particular type of science exam. Primary school teachers have a very different need: to develop a clear and focused understanding of the science in order to be able to teach it effectively to others.

    The idea of 'keeping one page ahead in the book' is now, surely, long gone. Teaching is much more than the passing on of facts for future regurgitation by a new generation of learners. Before teaching comes assessment and planning. Initial assessment is needed to reveal the children's ideas, to find out what they know and what they don't. Once you move on to finding out what their level of understanding is, things start to become less clear, but this is necessary in order to find out where the learning should start. After assessment comes planning: deciding on the ideas that you want the children to develop and the challenges, tasks and questions that you expect will get them there. Finally, there is the delivery: the teaching and learning that will see the plans come to fruition. Such a process can be embedded in the science curriculum for a key stage, or can be part of a pupil/teacher interaction lasting a few seconds. The key is understanding where the children are, where they need to go next and how to get them there – that is, understanding the science.

    This book does not try to give you all the scientific facts you will ever need as a teacher. That's impossible: science is changing far too quickly. What it will attempt to do, largely through clear explanations, models and analogies, is to help you to reach a better understanding of the science – to help you visualize what is happening. Some of the science has been simplified in an attempt to clarify the ideas, but every effort has been made to ensure that the material is scientifically correct.

    POCKET GUIDES: LIFE PROCESSES

Structure of this book

Each area of science is broken down into a few **key concepts**. These are the ideas used as a focus for the development of explanations and examples. Together they form the basis of the elements within each strand of science of which children (and consequently you) need to develop a secure understanding.

A **concept chain** is included to provide a clear indication of progression and development. The chain goes beyond Key Stage 2, in order to help you see where the children are going. Scientific understanding is a never-ending quest; but an appreciation of where a child is in the learning continuum allows previous points to be reinforced and the next ones to be explored. With any scheme of work, a sense of place and direction is essential for all concerned.

The **subject facts** provided have three main purposes:
● To help you understand the ideas so that you can teach them effectively. (The explanations will often go beyond what you need to teach at Key Stage 2.)
● To show where the children will be going next with their learning.
● To make it easier for you to identify where the children have developed misconceptions.
Connected to this is a list of the important technical **vocabulary** that will be required to teach and understand these key ideas. It is especially important for the children to realize that some words used in general conversation have particular and explicit meanings in science, and to begin to appreciate when they need to apply this scientific usage.

Children are generally fascinated by **amazing facts**. Each scientific theme includes a few with which you can impress the class. They are mostly chosen to give some idea of the scale or extremes within the topic.

An understanding of some **common misconceptions** and what you might do about them is important in both assessment and planning. If you are aware of ways in which children might hold misconceptions, you can plan activities in such a way that children holding these ideas can be identified. Focused teaching can then be effectively employed. This section offers advice on identifying and rectifying pupil misconceptions.

Some common **questions** that children frequently ask about the phenomena and processes within particular areas of science are presented, together with suggestions on how they can be answered to give children an understanding of the science involved. However, the answers may not always provide a full explanation!

Further ideas for practical **teaching activities** are provided, with a focus on particular approaches (exploring, investigating, sorting and classifying) and on the use of ICT to enhance learning. Where possible, specialist science equipment is avoided. This helps to link the science to familiar and practical contexts. However, in some cases particular equipment is necessary for measuring or collecting, or is required for health and safety reasons. The ICT activities depend on a certain level of hardware and software availability: word and data processing facilities; the ability to capture sound and images and incorporate them into presentation software; remote data capture (for example, temperature probes). The use of the Internet should be encouraged; but reference to it is restricted here because of the transitory nature of many websites.

Approach to teaching and learning

This book leans towards a particular learning theory – without, I hope, slavishly following it. The constructivist approach to the teaching of science has developed over many years, and is now acknowledged as a highly effective way of ensuring that children develop scientific abilities on the basis of a secure foundation in scientific concepts. Constructivism attempts to avoid teaching children an understanding of a scientific process or phenomenon while, at the same time, allowing them to continue to hold a conflicting conception. It is easy for a child to believe two very different explanations for the same concept concurrently. They may have been told one explanation at school, and use it to respond when the teacher asks; but hold another, arising from their empirical observations, which they use the rest of the time (for example, 'Plants go to sleep at night').

To adopt a constructivist approach, the teacher must first determine the area of science that the children will need to work within (from the curriculum or the school's scheme of work). This will help the teacher to identify the range of ideas and misconceptions that the children might hold. Next, the teacher needs to identify a stimulus or context which will help the children to focus on the topic by engaging their interest in something familiar. The next three stages depend on the children. In the first stage, the stimulus or context is used to elicit the children's ideas, with the teacher questioning and probing to discover the extent of their understanding. Based on this assessment, the teacher plans a range of highly focused activities, building on the children's questions and suggestions to reinforce correct ideas and challenge misconceptions. In a final assessment and reflection stage, the children are asked to consider how their understanding has changed. The teacher acknowledges progression and identifies the next steps to be taken.

This approach is about constructing a secure understanding of science based on broad and firm foundations, rather than requiring the children to retain transitory knowledge which they are unable to link to any pre-held ideas. However, there is a downside. This approach tends to take longer, both in the meeting of individual learning objectives and in terms of the coverage of content, than a more piecemeal approach. Although 'finding out where the children are starting from' is an essential prerequisite, it could mean that the teacher is attempting to help the children progress from many different starting points. Applying probing questions to a whole class cannot be done both accurately and quickly – though if you have found a way, please get in touch! The recording of assessments is also very time-consuming, although it can be very satisfying to look back and register the progression. The teacher will need to group children with similar ideas, and find an efficient way of charting misconceptions and progress.

Not only is constructivism a highly effective way of teaching children, it also encourages a reflective and professional approach from the teacher. It leads the teacher to examine and analyse every step of the teaching; this will aid the development of a better understanding of the individual children and their learning, as well as of the scientific ideas and the means of communicating them.

This book is dedicated to Martine, William and James, who have continually asked me 'why' during the writing of this book – admittedly, mostly in the context of asking 'Why haven't you finished writing that book yet, Dad?'

Chapter 1

WHAT IS LIFE?

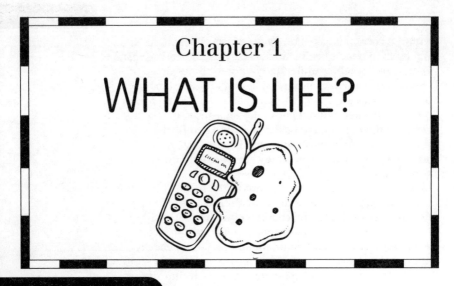

The ideas contained in the primary curriculum about 'the nature of life' are fundamental to our understanding of all biological aspects of science. However, while 'life' might appear at a surface level to be a straightforward concept to define, the closer you look, the more involved it becomes. This chapter attempts to provide clear scientific (as opposed to dictionary) definitions by which to classify life. One of the key problems with developing conceptual understanding in this area is the need to remember both common usage and scientific definitions of terms, and to know when to use each. The key ideas to be developed here are:

1. Life processes, common to all living things, can be used as a means of defining life.
2. Everything can be divided into 'living', 'no longer living' and 'never lived'.
3. Living things can be arranged into a broad classification system involving five 'kingdoms'.

Life concept chain

It is important to be aware of how these concepts of life might be developed. Below, you can follow **one** way in which this progression can be traced. It goes up to Key Stage 3 because it is necessary to know where the children will be going next. A useful way to demonstrate your own understanding of the concepts is to produce your own concept chain.

KS1

All living things, including human children, share a set of common characteristics. Animals are a type of living thing. Humans are a type of animal. All animals have the ability to move, feed, grow, reproduce and sense the world around them. Plants are another form of living thing, different from animals. Some things have never been alive; they have never been able to do what living things can do.

KS2

Living things die and cease to be able to do the things they could do while they were alive. All living things need to gain energy through nutrition in order to grow and reproduce. Plants share several characteristics of living things with animals; both grow and reproduce and require nutrition, but they perform these characteristics in different ways. Plants are not able to move or sense their environment in the same way as animals. Plants and animals are not the only forms of life on Earth. Animals and plants can be divided into smaller sub-groups according to their characteristics. The class of animal to which humans belong is the mammals.

KS3

Time and the degree of change from their living form are important factors in deciding whether an object was once alive or has never lived. As well as the living kingdoms of plants and animals, there are also fungi, micro-organisms without nuclei (such as bacteria), and simple-structured organisms with nuclei (such as algae). These kingdoms can be subdivided to a point where a species is defined as a set of living things that are able to reproduce viable young.

Concept 1: Defining 'living things'

Life processes

Certain basic life processes are common to all living things, and distinguish them from non-living things. Living things:
● grow – they also have a life cycle, which includes death (ceasing to exist as a living thing)
● reproduce – they have a system by which they produce others like themselves

Subject facts

● use energy – they require an energy source, either direct (from sunlight) or indirect (by eating another organic entity).

Some non-living things meet one or two of these criteria, but never all three. A salt crystal will grow and extend its crystalline structure, but not reproduce. Clouds can grow (expand) and die (dissipate), and require an energy source (the Sun) to evaporate the water; but they cannot reproduce. All living things – at least, all that we are currently aware of – are based upon carbon compounds. Many other chemicals are involved as well, but all living things on this planet can be defined as 'carbon-based life forms'.

In the simplest living things, growth and reproduction can be almost indistinguishable. A single-celled entity is a single-celled entity: it never grows beyond this. When it has absorbed sufficient energy and become a slightly bigger single-celled entity, it divides to become two single-celled entities; each is an exact replica of the other. If there is not enough suitable energy available, it becomes dormant or dies. Its whole existence is based around making more of itself. Which is precisely what humans, at the other end of the evolutionary scale, are here to do – they just find other, diverting activities to perform as well.

Many living things on Earth contain chemical substances which enable them to **photosynthesize** energy directly from sunlight. This energy is used to convert chemicals (carbon dioxide and water) into organic matter (sugars). All other living things (apart from a certain group of soil bacteria) use these photosynthesizing organisms, either directly or indirectly, as a food source. (For more about photosynthesis, see Chapter 5, page 121.)

'Living' and 'alive'

These words are often poorly used in common speech, which can lead to misunderstanding when the scientific concept of life is discussed. There are many different forms of living things. They all have common features, but these are sometimes quite difficult to appreciate. In the same way, it can be quite difficult to distinguish between living and non-living things.

It is only by observing familiar living things that we come to understand what is meant by 'alive'. By repeating language within particular contexts, we begin to associate a collection of partially-defined characteristics with the concept of 'life'. This is in much the same way that we begin to appreciate that 'table' is a particular concept:

though it may appear in many different shapes or materials, we are usually able to recognize an object as a 'table'. If you sit on a coffee table, does it become a bench? At what point does the definition change? We have similar problems in defining 'life'.

The criteria for life described above work well enough in most circumstances, but challenges to those criteria can help us either to reinforce the concept or to adjust the definition. Two examples challenge the concept of 'living' quite well: fire and grass seeds.

Superficially, fire seems to meet the criteria for life quite well. It needs oxygen to convert fuel into energy; it can grow and die; it can start lots of little fires. So is it alive? Well, no. For all other living things, you need to start off with a living thing. You cannot create life where there was no life before, but you can create fire where there was no fire. Fire is a sustainable chemical reaction which occurs where the conditions are favourable. Life is much more than that.

A grass seed, though, does not present any of the characteristics of life – so does that mean it is not alive? Basically, a seed is a store of energy and a set of genetic instructions that tell it to grow when the conditions are right. A seed can stay in this inactive or **dormant** condition for a long time, and still be capable of growth. Could it be argued that coal is fire in a dormant condition? All it needs is the right conditions for it to turn into fire. However, coal lacks any built-in instructions which would enable it to develop in a distinctive way. The burning of coal is purely a chemical reaction which follows predictable and unchanging rules.

'We are star dust...'

The point at which a living thing ceases to be alive is quite difficult to determine. In relation to human life, there is an ongoing debate: legal, medical and religious groups argue about the point at which life begins and ends, while technology attempts to extend the limits of both.

Nor is death the end of organic change. After a living thing has died, it begins to decay and become less like a living thing. Cut grass is recognizable as something that was once alive, but leave it long enough in the right conditions and it will change into peat. In this form, it is still recognizable as being organic material. If it is compressed and left for several million years, it changes into a rock called coal. Should coal be described as 'once alive' or as 'never alive'? 'Once alive' would seem to be more appropriate – but how many other rocks are like this? Chalk was once the shells of tiny marine animals, and so was once alive. When chalk is heated and squashed by other rocks, its structure will be compressed and it will turn into a much harder rock called marble. Does this mean that a marble statue of a horse was once alive?

If we did not draw a line somewhere, we would be forced to conclude that the air around us was once alive: much of it must surely, at one point or another, have been breathed in and so have been part of a living thing. It is generally accepted that once ex-living material has been turned into rock or broken down into its constituent chemical components, it is no longer classified as 'once living' but is classified as 'never alive'. A deceased vole can be described as 'once living', but after decomposers (organisms that reduce living material to its chemical components) have been at it, it will have been reduced to chemicals within the soil that are regarded as 'never alive'.

Why you need to know these facts

Life and living processes are what separate biology from other areas of scientific study. The classification of a thing as 'alive' or 'living' is fraught with difficulties, so it is important that the criteria for life are understood and explained carefully. The line between living and non-living may seem a very clear one – but if that were so, why do theologians and lawyers continually spend so much time and effort attempting to define it in relation to humans? The use of the word 'living' in so many different contexts, such as 'living-flame gas fire' and 'the living planet', widens its usage dramatically.

The wording used in the National Curriculum is a gross simplification of the scientific issues. Although there is clearly no need to go into the depth explored above with primary-age children (this is likely to cause even greater confusion), knowing where their understanding will eventually lead them is important for making sure that they keep 'on track'.

Vocabulary

Alive or **living** – displays all of the characteristics of a living thing (growth, energy use, reproduction).
Dormant – has the potential for life when the environmental conditions are suitable.
Never alive – contains no material that was once alive (unless that material has since changed significantly in chemical structure and composition).

● Grass seeds found in the pyramids of Egypt have been planted and successfully grown after lying dormant for up to 4000 years.

● Coal, oil and gas have formed from the remains of vegetation and microscopic animals that died hundreds of millions of years ago.

All things that move are living

Common misconceptions

From the inaccurate use of language in TV and other media (for example, 'If it moves, kill it!'), some children can develop the idea that all things that move can be classified as living – including flames, cars and household machinery. Popular superstitions about cars and other machines having 'a life of their own' do not help. In these cases, it is important to help the children to redefine their understanding of 'alive' in line with the scientific view by stressing the criteria for life. Explain that a machine may be constructed to move like a living thing, but is not alive.

Is there life on other planets?

Questions

The generally accepted answer among the scientific community is 'Yes, probably... but we are not really sure.' Given the advances in carbon-based chemistry over the last ten years, it is not beyond the realms of possibility for 'life' (meaning simple strands of a self-replicating DNA-like substance) to be artificially designed and produced within the next hundred years. If we are able to create it, the likelihood of life arising by chance on another planet (orbiting another star) seems greater. However, given that the conditions may be entirely unlike those on Earth when life formed here, the life forms that arise on another world may be virtually unrecognizable to us. In the words of Mr Spock: 'It's life, Captain, but not as we know it!'

Are cut flowers alive?

They can still perform some basic functions – for example, the flowers will open and close. If they are provided with appropriate conditions (water and some warmth and light), they will continue for several days in a 'fresh' state. In addition, some plants are able to regrow from cuttings: the cutting will develop a new root system and become a whole, living plant. But the general answer must be 'No': a flower head is a detached part of a plant that can be preserved in appropriate conditions, but cannot grow.

Similarly, if you were to cut off a human finger, it could be preserved in a viable state (allowing time for it to be reattached). Fresh blood could be circulated through it, and electrical pulses could be passed through it to stimulate the nerves and muscles in order to make it move – but it would not be capable of independent life.

Is it really dead?

'Dead' and 'dormant' are very different states. Seeds may appear dead – there's no obvious sign of life – but given the right conditions, they will start to grow. Death is when all life processes cease and cannot be restored. Although humans have been revived after immersion in very cold water and have been without a heartbeat for more than two hours, it is not something to try at home! Death is irreversible and permanent, not to be confused with sleep or inactivity.

Teaching ideas

Living and non-living things (sorting, explaining)

Provide a collection of objects (or pictures of objects) and ask the children to sort them into 'living' and 'non-living'. As they do so, ask them to justify their decisions. The objects will need to be familiar ones, so that the children are immediately aware of their characteristics. Extend this by asking them to divide the 'non-living' category into 'once lived' and 'never lived'.

Concept 2: Classifying living things

Subject facts

Levels of classification

To get from 'It is a living thing' to 'It is a human' requires at least seven levels of classification. The process of classification is progressive, going through a sequence of levels:

● **Kingdom** – this describes the cell structure and organization (and for multicellular organisms, describes how energy is obtained). The **animal** kingdom is defined as: multicellular, non-photosynthetic organisms that co-ordinate using nerves.

● **Phylum** – the differentiation of different groups at this level and beyond depends on the content of the particular kingdom. Humans belong to the phylum **chordates**, which have a nerve cord and brain within a spine and skull.

● **Class** – humans belong to the class known as **mammals**, which have milk-bearing glands for their young and have internal fertilization.

● **Order** – the **primates**, the order to which humans belong, are those animals possessing an opposable thumb.

● **Family** – humans belong to the family of **anthropoids**, which contains monkeys and apes but not lemurs.

● **Genus** – these are closely similar in appearance. Apart from human beings, all members of the genus *Homo* are now extinct.

● **Species** – members of a species are so closely related that breeding between them is possible. In this case, all human types or races belong to the species *Homo sapiens*.

The five kingdoms

Children at Key Stages 1 and 2 only need to know much about two of the five kingdoms: plants and animals. **Plants** are defined as those multicellular, photosynthetic organisms whose cell walls contain cellulose – that is, green plants with clearly defined leaves or stems (such as trees, grass and moss). For a definition of **animals**, see above.

Two other kingdoms that deserve a mention are **fungi** and **prokaryotes**. The latter are usually referred to as 'micro-organisms' or 'bacteria'. Fungi are **decomposers**: they gain their nutrients by assisting with the decay of dead organic matter. They perform this recycling task alongside certain types of **bacteria** (a large group within the prokaryote kingdom), which also gain their nutrients from decaying organic materials.

Prokaryotes

The main difference between the kingdoms of fungi and prokaryotes is that fungi tend to be multicellular organisms, whereas prokaryotes (being a much simpler form of life and lacking a nucleus to their cells) are not. Another difference is that prokaryotes are not all decomposers – there are many different forms, classified according to the way they gain their carbon (from which all living things on Earth are made) and energy.

Autotrophic bacteria obtain their carbon from carbon dioxide, **heterotrophic** bacteria from organic material (compounds containing carbon, hydrogen and oxygen). The energy that they use to turn the carbon into replicas of themselves can be obtained either from light (the Sun) or from chemicals. Those that use light (**photoautotrophs**) include bacteria which live in the ocean and oxygenate the water, and also provide a foundation for the food chain in the seas. Some bacteria that use chemicals as a source of energy (**chemoheterotrophs**) can use organic material as both an energy and a carbon source. These variations mean that bacteria, which are the most ancient form of life on Earth, are found almost everywhere. They perform a huge range of functions in human life: some cause illness, while others are a source of antibiotics and other life-preserving drugs; some are important in processing food, others in processing effluent.

Low-life

Possibly the least well-known of the kingdoms is the collection of living things called 'protoctista'. These differ from prokaryotes in one very significant respect: their cells have a nucleus. This means that they are one step up on the evolutionary ladder, but they are still just single cells (or simple collections of similar cells). They rely on light as a source of energy, but they have not developed specialized cells (to form roots, leaves or stems) – this is what separates them from plants.

The classification of the protoctista kingdom is made more difficult by one of its best-known groups, algae, being shared between the prokaryote and protoctista kingdoms. **Cyanobacteria** (commonly known as 'blue-green algae') lack a nucleus to their cells, and so are a member of the prokaryote kingdom. Green, red and brown algae have nuclei in their cells, and so belong to the protoctista kingdom. These latter three forms of algae are commonly known as seaweed, kelp and pond scum.

There is an interesting little group of living things called **lichens**. These represent a **symbiotic** relationship between two types of organism: an alga and a fungus. The alga produces a type of carbohydrate which the fungus uses as a foodstuff; in return, the fungus protects the alga from the extremes of the environment by retaining moisture. As an example of teamwork, it seems to work well: there are 15 000 known types of lichen.

Plants and animals

Now we come to the kingdoms most frequently used to represent living things, particularly during the primary phase of education. **Plants** are multicellular organisms that **photosynthesize** (gain energy from light), and whose cell walls are made rigid by containing **cellulose**. **Animals** are also multicellular organisms; but unlike plants, they do not photosynthesize. This description would place them in the same group as fungi – so two additional characteristics, the use of egg production in reproduction and co-ordination through specialized nerve cells, complete the distinction.

Plants

Plants are divided into six distinct groupings or phyla. The most familiar is the phylum of 'flowering plants' (which is discussed in detail in Chapter 5, as it forms the focus of work on plant life at Key Stages 1 and 2). **Ferns** and **gymnosperms** (conifers and palms) are the other 'vascular' plant groups. **Vascular plants** are those with internal 'transport systems' for water and nutrients. **Non-vascular plants** make up the other three phyla: mosses, liverworts and hornworts. These plants do not have long roots which they can send down into the ground in search of water, and so can only grow on moist surfaces where they are in direct contact with water.

Ferns are some of the most ancient forms of plant life. They dominated the landscape in the Carboniferous period (300 million years ago), and formed the major part of the diet of the first dinosaurs. Most ferns are recognizable by their thin, feathery leaves or fronds – but only in a certain phase of their lives. Ferns have a two-stage life cycle. Firstly, the recognizable plant produces **spores** by simple cell division. These spores **germinate** and develop into plants that often have a small, flat, heart-shaped structure containing male and female parts. In the presence of water, these parts combine to produce a fertilized **seed**, which grows into the familiar fern plant.

Gymnosperms (literally 'naked-seed' plants), including conifers and cycads (palms), have also existed since ancient times. Cycads were the dominant form of plant life in the Jurassic period (200–150 million years ago). These plants are thought to have evolved from ferns. They tend to be woody (trees and bushes), and they grow directly from seeds. The seeds grow in protective **seed cones**: structures of woody scales that respond, when ripe, to the moisture content of the air, so that the seeds are released when the growing conditions are most favourable. Although most of the cycads (the most ancient form of gymnosperm) have become extinct, the conifers are still going strong.

Animals

Figure 1 shows a 'family tree' or branching classification of the major types of animal. The animal kingdom contains over 30 phyla – although most of them are fairly obscure,

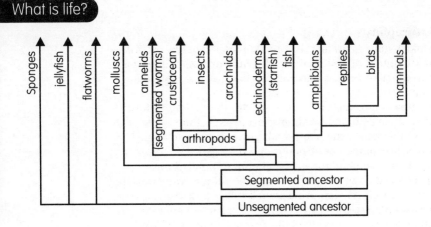

marine-dwelling forms. There are at least 12 different phyla used to classify what a non-biologist would call 'worms' – but any one of these phyla has less in common with the others than we do with a goldfish. The three animal phyla most commonly referred to are:

● **Molluscs** – unsegmented animals with a muscular foot, and often with a shell (snails, slugs, shellfish and others).

● **Arthropods** – segmented animals with a jointed **exoskeleton** (insects, spiders, crabs and others).

● **Chordates** – animals with an internal bony skeleton, a skull-encased brain and a nerve cord (fish, amphibians, reptiles, birds, mammals).

The diversity of species within each phylum is highly variable. At one extreme, there is a microscopic marine animal so different from anything else that its species has a phylum of its own (called placozoa, or *Trichoplax adherens* to its friends – though clearly it doesn't have many). At the other extreme, there are over one million species of arthropods (by comparison, there are only 45 000 species of chordates). Many of the marine animals can only be distinguished from plants because they don't photosynthesize. Sponges, for example, are a very basic animal life form: they lack any distinct internal organs, rely on water flow for feeding and movement, and remain attached to a rock for most of their life cycle.

The terms **vertebrate** and **invertebrate** are commonly used in describing animals, but are not really accurate enough for biological classification. Some marine animals could be placed in both categories at different times in their life cycle. Using the term 'with/without a central nerve cord' would be slightly more accurate (not all spinal cords are surrounded by a backbone).

Arthropods

This phylum is subdivided into five main classes, according to the number of body segments and legs (and where the legs are attached). All arthropods have segmented bodies with jointed legs. By far the biggest class of arthropods are the **insects**, which have more species than all other forms of animals combined. Other arthropods include **crustaceans** (lobsters and crabs), **arachnids** (spiders, mites, scorpions), **centipedes** and **millipedes**. This phylum represents some of the oldest animal forms that have specialized body parts. In evolutionary terms, they were the first to develop limbs, wings, heads, eyes and a few other useful little bits. They are also notable for the **metamorphosis** (change in form) that some species go through during their life cycles.

Chordates

This phylum, to which humans belong, can cause quite a few difficulties in terms of classification. Because it contains the animals that are most closely related to us, this phylum has been subject to the greatest level of study over the years – resulting in the greatest degree of reclassification as definitions have become more precise. Due to their familiarity, many of the terms have slipped into common usage, leading to double meanings for some of the key vocabulary. **Fish**, for example, do not make up a distinct scientific class, but rather three classes.

Fish

The first class of fish, **chondrichthyes** (cartilaginous fish), include fish that have a cartilage skeleton, fleshy fins and a mouth that is backward of a snout (ventral). The second class, **osteichthys** (bony fish), have bony skeletons, fins supported by bony spines and a mouth that comes at the very front of the body. The third class are the jawless fish (such as eels), which are generally long and thin and have sucker-like mouth openings with tongues.

The first two classes represent the types that children are most likely to be familiar with, an example of each being the great white shark and the mackerel. Bony fish are more highly evolved, having developed a **swim bladder** which means that they do not need to keep swimming to avoid sinking. The swim bladder eventually evolved into lungs for air breathing as fish evolved as the ancestors of reptiles, amphibians, birds and mammals. Fish were the dominant and most evolved form of animal life during the Devonian period (400–360 million years ago).

Amphibians

Apart from some forms of lungfish that were able to survive on land for short periods of time, the **amphibians** (such as frogs, newts and salamanders) were the first class of animal to be able to breathe air for extended periods. They are defined by the way that they **metamorphose** from gill-breathing young to lung-breathing adults, usually only returning to the water to breed. Their numbers have declined dramatically since their heyday during the Carboniferous period (360–290 million years ago). Currently they are the class of animal that is decreasing in numbers most rapidly, with significant numbers of deformed adults (with extra limbs and so on) being discovered, possibly as a result of pollution. (See Chapter 2, page 39.)

Reptiles

Reptiles developed from amphibians around the end of the Carboniferous period. They continued as the dominant life form – particularly the branch that evolved into the dinosaurs – until the end of the Cretaceous period (65 million years ago), a period of over 200 million years. However, they were subject to several mass extinctions during the Cretaceous period, the last leaving just four of the 23 orders known to have existed – the dinosaurs being the most famous casualty. Lizards, snakes, turtles, tortoises and the crocodilians are now the main representatives of this class.

The reptiles' great advance from the amphibians was the hardened shell of their eggs, which allowed reproduction out of water to take place and so removed the need for a metamorphosis from infant to adult. For added protection, they have a scaly skin. It should be noted that not all reptiles lay eggs: some give birth to live young, though they do not feed them by producing milk like mammals.

Mammals and birds

These two classes are distinct from the others in this phylum in that they are able to regulate their own body temperatures. Although they are known as 'warm-blooded', this is not very precise (nor is 'cold-blooded' for the others), as the blood of all chordates tends to be quite warm. The better term is **endotherm**, which means that they control their body temperature from within. The other chordate classes are **ectotherms**, which means that they rely on the environment to regulate their body temperature. (See Chapter 2, page 35.)

Mammals are distinct from any other form in that the female has mammary (milk-bearing) glands with which to rear their young. They evolved slowly from reptiles, becoming a separate class about 200 million years ago; but it wasn't until the extinction of most reptilians (about 65 million years ago) that they began to prosper. There are three mammalian sub-classes, based upon the mode of reproduction. The monotremes (egg-layers) are representative of the most primitive form of mammals – the duck-billed platypus is a well-known example. Next came the marsupials, which give birth to partially developed young; and then the placentals, which produce live and immediately viable offspring to be fed from the mammary glands. The mammalian class will be the main focus of Chapter 3.

Birds are thought to have evolved about 150 million years ago from dinosaurs, along with many species that flourished alongside the dinosaurs during the late Cretaceous period. Most of these died out at the same time as the dinosaurs; but the bird class was able to re-establish itself, and most current families of bird can be traced back about 50 million years. Birds are egg-laying endotherms with one pair of wings instead of front legs. Their bodies are covered in feathers: lightweight structures with a hollow stem and fine strands. These are thought to have evolved from scales.

Birds have turned out to be particularly difficult to classify. Those that have been assigned to the same groups according to external features and habitat have not been confirmed as near-relatives by DNA sampling. For example, the vultures of the Americas, according to DNA analysis, appear to be more closely related to storks than to African vultures. Overall, about 25 orders of birds have been defined to distinguish such types as swimming birds, wading birds, perching birds and flightless birds.

Humans

All humans belong to the same species of mammal: they can interbreed. It is very likely that humans evolved in a single place and then, over a period of hundreds of thousands of years, spread themselves across the Earth. Ice ages (glacial dislocations) and changing sea levels were the likely causes of various groups of humans becoming isolated from others, leading to the development of races in different parts of the world. It is quite possible, with mass transport now freely available, that distinct human races will have disappeared by the next millennium.

Why you need to know these facts

Once the decisions about what is living and what is not have been made, you are left with an amazingly diverse category called 'living things'. As humans (and in particular scientists) have a predilection for sorting and classifying, there is a need for further, more clearly defined categories. The 'five kingdoms' classification system, with its subdivisions, is the one that is currently in favour and will be used for the foreseeable future – though it is likely to be tinkered with constantly! Working with younger children, you will only ever have to use very broad descriptions; but to avoid errors, it is important to have an overview of the whole classification system.

Vocabulary

Endotherm – an animal with internal control of its body temperature.
Ectotherm – an animal with no internal control of its body temperature.
Kingdom – the major classification of different groups of living organisms.
Phylum – the first step down in classification from a kingdom. A phylum gathers together organisms that share major structural features.
Species – a group of living things that are so closely related that viable interbreeding is possible.
Animals – multicellular organisms that co-ordinate movement through nerve impulses.
Plants – multicellular photosynthesizing organisms.
Prokaryotes – micro-organisms (including **bacteria**) that lack a cell nucleus.

Amazing facts

● Prokaryotic cells range in size from 0.0001mm to 0.003mm. If you stacked 10 000 of the smallest prokaryote in a pile, they would reach almost 1mm into the air. If you did the same with 10 000 elephants, you would have a tower 34km tall – four times the height of Mount Everest. You would also have some unhappy elephants near the bottom.
● All of the larger animals, including humans, need bacteria in their gut to help them digest food – there are millions of living things inside you.
● All of the chordates (more commonly known as vertebrates) combined make up less than 1% of the total number of animals living on this planet. At the other extreme, there are more arthropods than all other animals put together.

All animals have four legs and are furry.
This is a common misunderstanding caused by the misuse
of the word in everyday speech. Often the word 'animal' is
used where 'mammal' would be more appropriate. There
are two ways to correct this basic misconception. Firstly,
make sure that you use the term 'animal' correctly yourself
in order to model the usage for the children. Secondly, help
the children to accept that other people (usually older and
less scientifically knowledgeable than themselves) will use
other meanings of the word that the children should accept
and work with. Children need to understand that the term
'animal' can refer equally well to mammals, birds, fish,
insects, jellyfish, spiders and humans.

Humans are not animals.
Oh yes they are! This goes back to the previous point about
the use of the term 'animal' in common speech. 'Animal' is
often used as a derogatory term meaning 'lower form of
life', and children need to be aware of this double meaning
so that they are able to recognize it and not be confused.

Why are all living things sorted into groups?

Mainly because it makes it easier for people to identify
them and see how they are related. Knowing the name of
everything is very important to certain people (particularly
young children!), so being able to identify a creature by its
external features is a particularly useful approach. It is
certainly much more efficient than working through an
animal dictionary, starting with 'Does it look like an
aardvark?' and finally deciding that it best matches the
description of a zyzomys (Australian rock rat).

Sets (sorting, matching, classifying)

This is a key element of all activities to be carried out in
this section. Basic classifying activities can be carried out
using a wide variety of instructions and resources, and can
be approached at many different levels. The more
knowledgeable the children become, the more challenging
the activity can be. For example:
● Present a selection of plastic models of chordates (there
is no need to use that word) for the children to sort into
mammals, reptiles, amphibians, fish and *birds*. This is
clearly based more on what they already know than what
they can observe in detail.

● Carry out the same activity with pictures, allowing more detailed observation.
● The children can map the names of particular animals to the names or descriptions of the five chordate classes.
● They can map pictures of various living things to the plant and animal kingdoms.

Keys (observing, sorting, matching, classifying)

The use of keys to identify organisms is particularly important to the scientist. Children at Key Stage 2 should be encouraged to use and develop their own identification keys to cover a limited range of living things. This can start with simple games based on similarities and differences:
● 'Guess who?' The children identify a mystery animal by asking you questions about its key characteristics.
● 'Who am I?' Using a display of pictures of living things, the children have to work out which animal (or plant) you are by asking questions to which you can answer either *Yes* or *No* – for example, 'Can you breathe in the water?'
● The children can design sorting trees for a limited range of organisms which others can use to identify specimens.
● They can use computer software such as *Branch* to generate a sorting tree.

Similarities and differences (observing, sorting)

● Ask the children to look at another living thing (or a picture or video of it) and observe similarities and differences between it and themselves. Go on to discuss what they know about the other living thing. Note any further similarities and differences between it and the children that arise. Do any misconceptions appear?

Resources

The *Observer's Book of...* series (Godfrey Cave Associates) provides excellent information on (and, in some cases, identification keys for) a wide variety of living things.

The Natural History Museum (tel: 020 7942 5000) provides both excellent resources and a wonderful venue for an educational visit to explore classification issues.

Provide the children with a variety of samples of once-living and never-living things, including fossils.

Suitable multimedia encyclopaedias on the variety of living things include *Encarta* (Microsoft) and the Dorling Kindersley *Eyewitness Encyclopaedia of Nature* and *Encyclopaedia of Science*.

Chapter 2

VERTEBRATES

Vertebrates, or more accurately chordates (see page 21), only represent a small proportion of the different forms of animal in existence on this planet. However, since humans belong to this phylum, it contains our nearest relatives – and so provides examples of life forms that children can readily identify with, giving opportunities for more detailed study of particular aspects of adaptation, behaviour or development. The key ideas to be developed here are:

1. Marsupials are a special type of mammal that rear their young in a unique way.

2. Birds, through their beak and foot variations, demonstrate adaptation to particular feeding habits and lifestyles.

3. Reptiles, as ectotherms, rely on their environment to regulate their temperature.

4. Fish are able to extract oxygen from water in order to breathe.

5. Amphibians are transformed during their life cycle, enabling them to move from one kind of environment to another.

In this case, there is no particular 'concept chain' or line of conceptual development (see page 10). The examples discussed in this chapter were selected because of the way that they can be used to stimulate a sense of wonder at the variety of life on Earth. Although none of the key ideas in this chapter are explicitly required by the National Curriculum, each of them allows an insight into the diversity of animal life, showing how every ecological niche has been exploited by one form of life or another. It also provides an opportunity for children to explore the development of vertebrate life from its earliest forms.

Most of these points can be introduced during Key Stage 1 (particularly through work on birds and amphibians); but all offer opportunities for in-depth individual or group study, with excellent potential for display or presentation.

Concept 1: Marsupials

Subject facts

Distribution

Marsupials are a distinct branch of the mammalian tree. After first evolving in North America some 85 million years ago, they migrated to Australia (the oldest marsupial fossils that have been discovered there are about 25 million years old), where they developed in isolation from placental mammals until the arrival of humans 40 000 years ago. Now there is only one marsupial native to North America, a species of opossum, though there are still over 70 species in South America.

It is in Australia, New Guinea and Tasmania that the greatest variety of marsupials still exist. These include the kangaroo (which leaps on two legs), koala (a marsupial sloth), wombat (a burrowing marsupial similar to a large rodent) and opossum (a marsupial shrew).

Birth and development

Whereas placental mammals produce fully-formed live young that have grown to a viable level of development within a womb, marsupials go in for a two-stage development.

The first stage is within the mother's womb. The fertilized embryo is neither attached to the mother via a placenta nor encased in a shell: it is simply supplied by a yoke sac. After less than one month of growth, when the yoke sac is empty, the partially-formed marsupial will have to venture out of the womb. At this stage a kangaroo, for example, will not yet have developed eyes or back legs; but it will possess very strong forelimbs and a homing instinct.

The mother will lick down a track of fur from the opening of her womb to her pouch. Then, using its forelimbs, the embryo-like form (weighing less than 1g) will drag itself to the pouch and latch onto a nipple, gathering nourishment and developing further until it has grown sufficiently to start letting go of the nipple for increasing amounts of time.

The young kangaroo will stay in the pouch for several months before tentatively venturing outside. It will return to the pouch for nourishment, safety and comfort for some considerable time after that, until it is finally 'evicted' by its mother. Some species of opossum lack a pouch, so the young are left dangling from the nipple or grip onto the mother's back.

Why be a marsupial?

As well as being able to use a pouch as a sort of 'second-stage womb', some marsupials are able to practise an interesting form of family planning. Kangaroos living in semi-arid areas are able to delay egg release, and thus conception, until the environmental conditions are right. When there is a plentiful supply of food and water, mating can safely be allowed to take place. Once a baby kangaroo has made it to the pouch, the kangaroo can mate again – and hold the development of the embryo at an early stage until pouch space is available. Once the more mature infant begins to leave the pouch, the embryo is allowed to continue developing. It is possible for a female kangaroo to have young at three stages of development at the same time: one weaned, but still likely to seek comfort in the pouch; one in the pouch, attached to a nipple; and one in a suspended state in the womb.

This mode of reproduction provides another benefit for marsupials that find themselves prey to other animals. On the African savannah, a heavily pregnant wildebeest would be relatively easy prey for a big cat, because it would not be able to run away. A kangaroo, on the other hand, may be able to eject its largest pouch infant and make a dash for it, in the knowledge that another baby in the pouch is less than a month away from emerging.

Marsupial ecology

Until the arrival of placental mammals (humans in particular), the marsupials (together with some large, flightless birds) filled the ecological niches that placental mammals filled elsewhere. In prehistoric times there were giant kangaroos over 3m tall feeding on the leaves of large bushes. In more recent times (it may or may not be extinct), the thylacine (or Tasmanian wolf) preyed on smaller marsupials. There are kangaroos that live only in the canopy of rain forests, and wombats that live only on grassland.

This type of mammal is exotic enough to engage the interest of children, while providing an opportunity to explore an alternative evolution. Although not all marsupials are to be found in Australia, all the native mammals in Australia are marsupial – with two notable exceptions, the duck-billed platypus and the echidna or spiny anteater. These are both egg-laying **monotremes**. The breeding habits of marsupials provide an excellent example of an alternative mode of development.

In addition, marsupials are fascinating examples of **parallel evolution**: the forms of marsupial life in Australia resemble those of placental mammal life elsewhere, due to the evolution of species to fill a range of ecological niches (see Chapter 7, page 150).

Marsupial – a mammal that carries its young in a pouch, where it feeds and completes its development.
Monotreme – an egg-laying mammal.

● An Australian eastern grey kangaroo can leap over 13m in a single bound, and can reach speeds of up to 64km/h.
● The Virginia opossum can have up to 56 offspring at any one time – but with only 13 nipples, the young have to race to survive.
● The yapok (water opossum of South America) feeds by catching fish in rivers. The females have a waterproof seal to their pouches, so that their young won't drown.
● Bandicoots spend only 12 to 13 days in the womb, then have to make for a nipple in their mother's pouch when they are only 10mm long.

The koala is a bear.
It looks a little like a bear (at least a teddy bear), but that is where the link ends. It does not fill the same ecological niche as a bear: it is much closer to the sloth in that sense. Most importantly, it is a marsupial, which bears are not.

Why aren't there marsupials in other parts of the world?

Since placental mammals were able to migrate to the Americas, on the face of it there seems little reason why the marsupials couldn't have travelled the other way. The key reason is that placental mammals are more effective survivors, and tend to drive the marsupials to extinction wherever they compete for food. The placentals were subject to greater competition as they evolved; so when they met the marsupials, they were able to feed more effectively and so force the marsupials into extinction. Because Australia was isolated by ocean from the rest of the world while the placental mammals were still developing, none made it that far – until humans introduced them. Now rabbits, mice and rats that were introduced by settlers are driving some smaller marsupials to extinction – just as they did in many other parts of the world millions of years ago.

As this topic has been included to challenge more able children, the suggested tasks are research activities that can be performed using books, multimedia packages and the Internet.

Marsupial life cycle
Children can research and record information on the different stages in the life cycle of a marsupial, then present it in a visual form.

Comparisons
Children can draw life-sized outlines of newborn and adult marsupials and placental mammals, noting similarities and differences between the two.

Niches
Children can find placental animals similar to various marsupials in the ecological niche they occupy (that is, the way that they live and use resources). For example, what is the African equivalent of Australia's red kangaroo? (Probably the antelope or deer.)

Marsupial humans?
After researching the life cycles and habitats of marsupials, ask the children to consider the idea of humans becoming marsupials. What would be the advantages and disadvantages of this change?

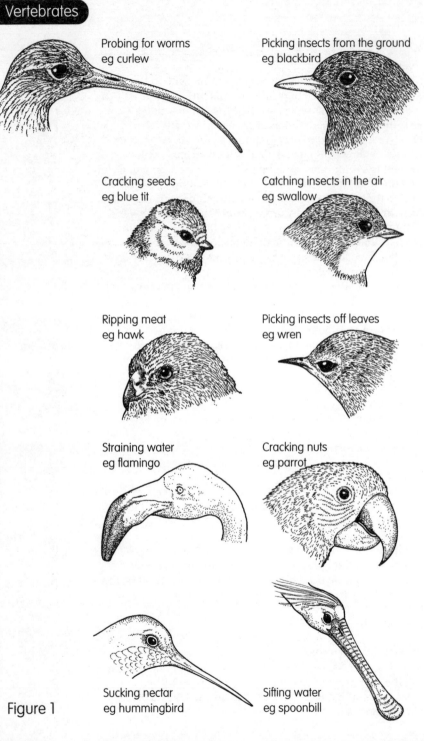

Probing for worms
eg curlew

Picking insects from the ground
eg blackbird

Cracking seeds
eg blue tit

Catching insects in the air
eg swallow

Ripping meat
eg hawk

Picking insects off leaves
eg wren

Straining water
eg flamingo

Cracking nuts
eg parrot

Sucking nectar
eg hummingbird

Sifting water
eg spoonbill

Figure 1

Beaks

The shape and size of a bird's beak (or bill) can provide an insight into its feeding behaviour (see Figure 1). A long, thin beak can be used to probe down into soft mud for food, while the greater leverage of a short, stocky beak is better for cracking open small seeds. With a little experience, it is possible to infer the probable diet of the bird from its beak.

By specializing in particular foodstuffs, birds become much more effective and efficient feeders – but this has to be balanced against the risks of becoming dependent on one kind of food. Very few species can survive for long if they are dependent on a single food source, unless that source is especially abundant: a change in the habitat might lead to the loss of their food source, and thus to extinction.

Feet

Just as the beak can tell you about the diet of a bird, the feet and legs can tell you things about its habitat and how it moves. They can be specially adapted for any one of several purposes, including perching, climbing, grasping prey, walking on mud, paddling or swimming (see Figure 2).

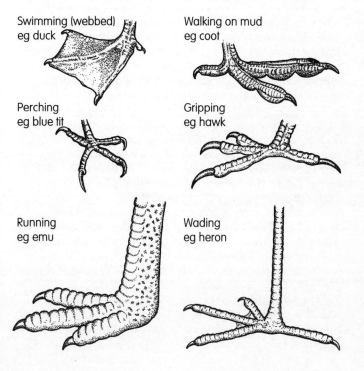

Swimming (webbed) eg duck

Walking on mud eg coot

Perching eg blue tit

Gripping eg hawk

Running eg emu

Wading eg heron

Figure 2

Ducks, who spend much of their time in water, tend to have short, powerful legs situated towards the rear of their bodies, with webbing between their toes. The domestic fowl (or chicken) is adapted to movement on land, as is the emu. But while the emu inhabits open spaces, the fowl (before it became domesticated) lived in semi-jungle areas; it has retained the ability to perch, and to fly up to its perch.

The tit can perch by locking its rear-facing toe into a gripping position, much as a hawk does in gripping its prey, but the hawk's talons are much more powerful. Like the emu, the heron has long legs; but they are much more slender since they don't need the power to run, only the length to keep the heron's body out of the water.

Why you need to know these facts

Birds provide many fine examples of the specialization of nature. By studying the beaks of birds, it is possible to determine quite a lot about their eating habits and, from that, the habitat in which they live. The design of their feet can also tell us a great deal about their lifestyle: Do they walk or swim? Grip or perch? Birds provide excellent material for a case study of adaptation for a purpose.

Vocabulary

Beak – an elongated appendage around a bird's mouth, made from a material similar to human fingernails.
Bill – a name given to a beak of the flatter (duck-like) type or the smaller (pigeon-like) type.
Talons – the grasping claws of a bird of prey.
Web – skin between toes to aid swimming.

Amazing facts

● The fastest-swimming bird is the gentoo penguin, which can swim at just over 27km/h. The human swimming record (over 50m) is almost 9km/h. The fastest-running bird is the ostrich, which can reach 65km/h. A human Olympic sprinter can run at 36km/h.
● The bills of some swifts are almost too small to be seen.
● The bill of the Australian pelican is over 45cm long. The bill of the sword-billed hummingbird, at 10cm, is longer than the rest of its body.

Common misconceptions

Only birds have beaks.
This is not quite true: there are a few other animals that use a beak (or rather, a bill) for specialized feeding, including aquatic mammals such as dolphins and the duck-billed platypus.

Do birds have teeth?

Strictly speaking, the answer is no. They rely on the sharpness of the edge of the beak to tear and cut. There are a few birds, such the merganser, which have a serrated edge to their beak – but this is not a true set of teeth. Nor is the 'egg tooth' that chicks break through their shell with a real tooth: it is just a sharp spike on the beak.

Food (identifying, inferring, sorting)

Teaching ideas

Ask the children to look at pictures of birds, assess the size and shape of their beaks, then sort the birds according to what they might eat. They can use books to check whether they were right.

Build a bird (identifying, inferring)

Give each group of children a different set of cut-out bird part shapes from the RSPB book *Variation and Adaptation*. Ask them to identify all the parts and assemble them to build a bird. From what they know about bird beaks and legs, can they say what food the bird might live off and what place it might inhabit?

Concept 3: In cold blood?

Subject facts

The first time that you handle a reptile can be a surprise: they are by no means cold. So where does this idea of the 'cold-blooded' reptile come from? In order to avoid having to cool their bodies by evaporation (sweating), reptiles, fish and amphibians regulate their internal temperatures by movement to a few degrees below that of the surrounding environment. In a reasonably warm environment, they are warm; in a cold environment they are cold.

So-called 'warm-blooded' animals function best within a narrow range of temperatures. They metabolize energy in their bodies at a high rate, releasing heat to maintain a constant body temperature. When they are too cold they shiver, increasing metabolism through muscle contraction. When they are too hot, they sweat or pant, evaporating more water to cool down.

The more correct terms (see page 22) are **endotherm** (temperature controlled from within) and **ectotherm** (temperature controlled externally). Endotherms require energy to control their metabolism in order to maintain a relatively constant temperature. As a result, they require more food than ectotherms. An ectotherm's level of activity depends on the ambient temperature: if it gets too cold, an ectotherm will become torpid and avoid movement. Within a particular temperature range, it will be at its most active. If it becomes too hot, it will have to adapt its behaviour once more and seek shade or shelter where it is cooler.

Why you need to know these facts

Reptiles are frequently referred to as 'cold-blooded' animals, which is technically untrue. Through coming to understand the inappropriateness of this term, the children will gain a valuable insight into the internal workings of animal bodies and their response to external conditions.

Amazing facts

Humans have a 'normal' body temperature of 37.5°C, but individuals have survived body temperatures as high as 46.5°C and as low as 16°C. However, an average person could expect to die of hypothermia with a core body temperature below 35°C, or of heatstroke with a temperature above 41°C.

Common misconceptions

'Cold-blooded' animals are cold to the touch.
It really depends on the environmental temperature. A fish pulled out of the Arctic Ocean will feel cold because its temperature will be near that of the water that surrounds it. A lizard picked up from the desert in daytime will feel hot for the same reason. The temperature of ectotherms varies with the temperature of their environment, whereas endotherms will attempt to remain at a constant temperature – though they may get colder at their extremities, where the blood circulation is less strong (which is why we need gloves and thick socks in winter).

Questions

So why are some animals called 'cold-blooded'?
In cold conditions, the blood temperature of an ectotherm blood will become noticeably lower than the temperature of human blood. Unlike humans and other endotherms, who will die if their core temperature falls too far below the

normal level, most ectotherms can survive extreme cold and revive when the environment warms up once more. Some fish can survive well in near-freezing waters, due to a natural 'anti-freeze' in their blood.

Were dinosaurs ectotherms, like lizards?

There is significant debate about whether the dinosaurs were ectotherms or endotherms. From the most recent research, it would seem that they developed from ectotherms to endotherms, or at least to having greater control over their metabolism, as they evolved. Studies of dinosaurs from different eras suggest that their metabolism speeded up, as towards the end of their 'reign' they became smaller and showed a greater need for activity to maintain their body temperature. This view is supported by fossilized skulls that show improvements to the teeth and nasal cavities, suggesting that the dinosaurs were becoming more efficient eaters.

Teaching ideas

● Most natural history programmes concerned with life in desert environments – very hot in the day and cold at night – will address the issue of activity and temperature in relation to snakes and lizards.
● The children can use books, multimedia CD-ROMs and the Internet to discover more about endothermic and ectothemic animals.

Concept 4: Water-breathing

Subject facts

Most fish spend their entire lives in water, with the water providing for all their needs. It contains the sources of food that they eat, supplies them with oxygen and maintains the temperature that they require. Oxygen dissolves readily into water: the action of waves on a beach causes oxygen in the air to be mixed into the water. Plants photosynthesizing underwater will also release oxygen.

Fish have developed **gills** to filter oxygen out of water in a similar way to the way our lungs filter oxygen out of air (see Chapter 3, page 57). The fish will take a gulp of water and then force the water out through slits in the sides of its head, causing the water to pass over its gills. The gills consist of many thin tissue surfaces or **membranes** that are full of blood vessels. As the water passes over these membranes, the oxygen is absorbed into the blood supply and carbon dioxide is passed into the water.

Some fish, such as tuna, are unable to gulp water and force it through their gills: they rely on a constant flow of water through their gills (caused by their own movement through the water) to breathe. If they stop swimming, they will not be able to breathe and will die.

Why you need to know these facts

Most children are aware that they inhale air. Some even appreciate that the most important part of air for breathing is oxygen. But when it comes to water-dwelling animals, confusion and misunderstanding sets in. Some animals dwell in the water but still need to surface for air; but what about those animals that live wholly in water – how can they breathe where we cannot? Understanding how gills work will help to clear up this confusion, and prepare them for later work on amphibian metamorphosis (see opposite) and on mammalian respiration (see page 53).

Vocabulary

Gill – a set of thin membranes that absorb oxygen out of water, allowing fish and other aquatic animals to 'breathe' underwater.

Amazing facts

● Sharks have to keep swimming in order to breathe – so they have to swim and sleep at the same time.
● The whale shark (which is a shark, not a whale) is the largest species of fish. It can grow up to 12.5m long.

Common misconceptions

Fish breathe water.
It's not water as such that the fish take in when they breathe: it's the oxygen that is mixed in to the water. In a similar sense, we take in the oxygen that is a part of the air. All animals require oxygen, and they extract it either from the mixture of gases that is air or from oxygenated water. It is basically the same respiratory process (breathing oxygen), but in a different medium.

Do lungfish breathe in water?

Young lungfish have external gills: feather-like organs that extract oxygen from the water. These degenerate with age and finally drop off, forcing the lungfish to surface in order to obtain oxygen from the air. Fish have an organ called a **swim bladder** which they can inflate by gulping in air; it helps them to maintain their buoyancy without having to swim all the time. In lungfish, this bladder has evolved the ability to absorb oxygen from air. They move around on land rather like eels or snakes. This is probably the way that all vertebrate air-breathing animals evolved.

Teaching ideas

Again, there are opportunities for further research using natural history videos, books, multimedia CD-ROMs and the Internet, focusing in particular on respiration in water and the structure of gills.

Concept 5: The metamorphosis of amphibians

Subject facts

Amphibians possess the ability to live in significantly different habitats, assuming a different form at different stages of their life cycle. Amphibians begin life as inhabitants of an aquatic world that are able to breathe in water; but as they mature and **metamorphose** into their adult form, they develop the ability to breathe air and move on land. This class of vertebrates was the first to conquer the land, and the fact that there are still many species around today shows how successful they have been.

Most amphibians return to water to lay their eggs. The eggs hatch into true aquatic animals, usually limbless and always with gills. This first stage of the life cycle may last for weeks or years, depending on the species. As most amphibians progress towards maturity, they will begin to develop limbs and lungs; some, like the frog, will even reabsorb their tails into their bodies. On reaching this mature stage, the amphibian will leave the confines of the water and move about on land. Some species of newt will live on land for a number of years, mainly keeping to damp areas, before returning to the water to breed.

Many of the more common frogs will progress through

four stages of development: first the **egg**, which hatches into a free-swimming aquatic **tadpole**; then a **froglet**, which has the beginnings of the adult frog's legs but still retains the tadpole's tail; and finally the mature **frog**, which is able to breathe. The fully aquatic stage of the development of an amphibian is also referred to as the **larva**.

Why you need to know these facts

Amphibians are the only group of 'higher' animals (apart from teenagers) that go through a fundamental change in their lifestyle, habitat and body shape as part of their natural development. Depending on availability and the ability of the school to provide an appropriate habitat, children can observe the changes in these animals as they happen. This demonstrates the idea of development (as opposed to growth) in a dramatic way.

Vocabulary

Tadpole – the larval, aquatic stage of a frog's development.
Larva – an immature stage of the life cycle.
Froglet – the stage of development of a frog which exhibits characteristics of both the tadpole and the mature frog.
Adult – the final stage of the life cycle, in which reproduction is possible.
Metamorphosis – a fundamental change in the body shape and lifestyle of an animal.

Amazing facts

● Frogs have webbed feet for swimming – but the 'flying frogs' of south-east Asia use their webbed feet to glide from tree to tree, or to parachute safely to the ground.
● The Mexican axolotl is an amphibian with external, feather-like gills. It looks like a pale adult newt – but in fact, it is the larval stage of a salamander. It can lose its gills and metamorphose into an air-breathing adult. I say 'can' because some axolotls do not metamorphose: some live their whole lives, including breeding, in the water.

Common misconceptions

Amphibians are cold and clammy.
Well, as most of them live near or in water, they do tend to be. But some, particularly toads, have a drier skin that gives them a warmer feel. Like all other ectotherms, they are the same temperature as their surroundings, so those that live in cold water will tend to be on the cool side, but in warm sunshine, they will be warmer.

Do all amphibians start life in water?

Not quite. Some frogs that live in particularly damp and humid parts of the tropics lay eggs on leaves, which hatch out directly into froglets.

Tadpoles (observing, recording)

This activity is only possible if you have access to a pond with frogspawn, so that tadpoles can be observed in their natural habitat. At regular periods during the spring and early summer, the children can observe the development of frogspawn into tadpoles and then froglets without disturbing them. They should **not** collect frogspawn for classroom observation. They can record and date the developments using drawings, photographs or a video camera. These could be transferred to a computer for inclusion in a multimedia presentation.

Life cycle displays (sequencing, presenting)

The children can prepare drawings, collect pictures or download images from the Internet to present displays on the life cycles of particular types of amphibian.

Resources

Reference books such as the *Observer's Book of...* (Godfrey Cave Associates) and *Spotter's Field Guide...* series (Usborne) are packed with useful facts.

Multimedia packages such as *Encarta* (Microsoft) and the Dorling Kindersley *Eyewitness Encyclopaedia of Science* and *...of Nature* are useful sources of images and information that could be incorporated into children's displays.

Some websites can be accessed via Encarta; others can be obtained via the usual search engines, using keywords such as:

● Marsupial
● Ectotherm
● Respiration in water
● Amphibian life cycle

Still and video cameras will be useful for recording observations of living things in their natural environment.

Chapter 3
MAMMALS

Key concepts

Most of the animal biology content of the primary science curriculum focuses very strongly on humans. This is perfectly reasonable, since humans are the animals of which children have the greatest experience and working knowledge! Those aspects of the curriculum that relate more specifically to humans (exercise, drugs, food groups and so on) are addressed in Chapter 4. However, the focus on humans must be balanced with an overall understanding that humans are simply one of many mammalian (let alone animal) life forms. Children need to realize that humans are mammals, sharing many of the same internal and external bodily systems with cats and horses. The definition of a mammal is dealt with in Chapter 1. The key ideas to be developed here are:

1. Many external body parts have specialized functions.
2. Mammals have an internal frame (skeleton) that provides protection and support.
3. The respiratory system causes energy to be released around the body.
4. Food must be broken down, both physically and chemically, before it can be absorbed into the body.
5. A nervous system transmits information around the body.
6. Energy is converted within muscles to allow movement of bones around joints in the skeletal structure.

7. Mammals use an array of specialized organs to sense their environment.

8. Mammals go through different stages of development within their life cycles.

Mammalian machine concept chain

For general comments on concept chains, see page 10.

KS1

All of a mammal's external body parts have particular names and functions. The same basic body part can be known by several different names (foot, hoof, paw, trotter and so on). Some of these body parts are concerned with movement. Some body parts allow information about the surroundings to be received (sensed). This information is received as sight, sound, smell, taste or touch. Food is needed by mammals for life, growth and activity. Mammals reproduce by giving birth to living babies.

KS2

Most mammals have similar body parts, though the names may differ from species to species. Some mammals (such as whales and bats) have very specialized body parts particularly suited to their environment. Systems of internal organs carry out specialized functions within the body such as digestion, respiration and circulation. The internal organs in these systems have particular names and functions. An internal skeleton of bone provides structure and allows movement. The skeleton protects key internal organs from injury. Muscles, joints and the skeleton combine to allow co-ordinated movement. The blood circulatory system conveys dissolved food, oxygen and waste products between the organs. Sense organs have specialized functions. Different mammals require different foods. Food is absorbed into the body through the process of digestion. Most mammals progress through five stages of development: infant, immature young, adolescent, adult and elderly. Mammals grow inside their mother until they are mature enough to survive. Infant mammals rely initially on their mother's milk for food.

KS3

The digestion system is a combination of related organs which progressively break down food into usable chemical components; these components are either used, stored for later use or ejected. The heart-lungs respiratory system allows external and internal gaseous exchange to take place. In muscles, the chemicals obtained from food (via digestion) are combined with the oxygen obtained from the air (through the lungs) to release energy and drive movement. The body's internal environment is constantly monitored and controlled to achieve stability through homeostasis. The menstrual cycle has a specific role in reproduction. Conception is the beginning of pregnancy.

Concept 1: What's that bit called?

Subject facts

For young children, the most intriguing aspect of studying the body is not conceptual development (it can be taken for granted that they will have at least some awareness of their own body parts) but the names by which the parts are known. Once children are aware that the part of their body where the eyes, ears, nose and mouth are is called the head, most will have little difficulty in transferring this idea accurately to most other mammals.

It is when the names children are expected to use change, as the need for a greater degree of scientific accuracy arises, that the problems begin to arise. At what stage do the words 'chest' and 'tummy' need to be replaced by 'thorax' and 'abdomen'? Is 'stomach' an acceptable alternative to 'tummy', when there is also an internal organ by that name? What is really the correct answer to the question 'How many fingers do you have?'

There are other areas of science where vocabulary in common usage can lead to confusion with the 'correct' scientific words or names, but probably none more so than here. So where do you start? One useful approach is to encourage the children to realize that, although there are specific names for every single part of every single type of mammal, we also have general words that are appropriate in most cases. For example, the general term 'foot' can cover a range of cases which are known specifically as 'trotter', 'paw', 'hoof' and so on.

Some names of body parts can be used for specific mammals, in particular humans; others can be applied equally to almost every mammal (see Figure 1). Having a standard set of names for body parts is useful: it allows us to share information more easily. If we were all to use different names for body parts, there would be utter

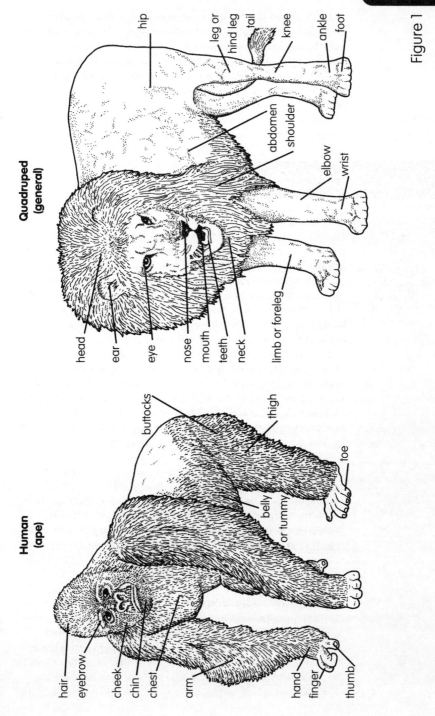

Quadruped (general)

hip

leg or hind leg

tail

knee

ankle

foot

abdomen

shoulder

elbow

wrist

head

ear

eye

nose

mouth

teeth

neck

limb or foreleg

Human (ape)

buttocks

thigh

toe

belly or tummy

hair

eyebrow

cheek

chin

chest

arm

hand

finger

thumb

Figure 1

confusion when it came to discussing the functions of various parts of the body. Having consistent terms for a given species will encourage the children to be consistent between species, so that there is a commonly understood terminology to which specific examples can be added (such as 'mane' or 'hoof') for particular cases.

'Scientific' terms

Terms such as 'abdomen' and 'thorax' only really need to be introduced at Key Stage 3; but some more able children, particularly if they are reading around the subject, searching multimedia packages or using the Internet, will find the use of more scientifically precise terms helpful. A search using the words 'tummy' or 'belly' probably won't get you very far – or might get you to places on the Web that you would rather not be – but 'abdomen', being a recognized scientific term, will focus on the cavity between chest and pelvis.

As happens when any database is searched, some terms prove to be more effective than others. Unfortunately, there are no 'hard and fast' rules about which words will work and which won't. Developing your own thesaurus for a particular database (such as *Microsoft Encarta*) is a very useful activity in its own right – and one that I've often found children are happy to perform, even as a 'homework' task.

Why you need to know these facts

Although the National Curriculum requires that children know the names of specific body parts, this must be regarded only as a first step. Having a common vocabulary as a basis for communication will enable children to develop an understanding of each named body part, including how it works and the purpose that it serves.

Since this is a purely vocabulary-based strand, we can move on directly to consider teaching ideas.

Teaching ideas

'Simon says' (identifying)

This is an old favourite that can be played by the youngest children, but can still cause amusement in groups of teacher training students ('Simon says touch your patella'). It provides a quick and easy means of assessing the level of anatomical knowledge of a whole class at once. I would suggest that the more able children are placed towards the back of the group (to prevent copying), and that you consistently get it wrong so the children are not able to copy you.

'Old MacDonald says' (identifying)

This is similar to the above, but the children have to point to named parts of stuffed toys or plastic model animals that they are holding. Be sensitive with your choice of animals so as not to conflict with any religious beliefs. This game is best played with a group of up to eight children: any more than that, and you will have difficulty seeing who is pointing to what. It also provides you with an opportunity to use species-specific language: if 'trotter' is called, for example, only those children holding model pigs will be able to point.

Matching and mapping (identifying)

Ask the children to match the names of body parts to blank labels on a model or diagram. This activity is easier to manage (and to store as evidence of attainment) if you use pictures and words on a sheet of paper; but models with coloured wool, word cards and Blu-tack or sticky tape can make an interesting alternative. Large-scale diagrams or models will make an excellent display – again, pictures are easier to manage, but large stuffed toys can be more effective. If you do use stuffed toys, be sensitive about how you attach them to the wall: watching a teacher pin a teddy bear to the wall with a staple gun can be a traumatic experience for a five year old! Also, keep the number of body parts identified to a reasonable level – seeing a teddy bear strapped to a display board by multiple strands of wool, like some kind of bizarre bondage ritual, can be a traumatic experience for a headteacher entering your classroom with a prospective parent.

Concept 2: Internal skeletal structures

Protection

Subject facts

Obviously, not all animals have their internal organs encased in a hard shell such as the exoskeleton of an arthropod. External blows can damage internal organs, and bone provides the first stage of an excellent impact protection system in mammals. The brain, which is rather exposed as an appendage at one end of the body, is almost completely encased in bone. The bones that fuse together to form the **skull** only join fully towards the end of infancy – a degree of suppleness allows the head of a baby to squeeze through the birth canal. Further 'impact protection' is offered by a liquid-filled sac that surrounds the brain and acts as a shock absorber.

The **rib cage** offers a semi-flexible protected area for many of the vital organs, particularly those concerned with respiration. The ribs are connected to the **sternum** at the front and the **spine** at the back, with one pair of ribs attached to each **vertebra** or spinal bone. Having ribs rather than a shell offers advantages in terms of both weight and movement. This flexibility can be felt while breathing. You can breathe either by pushing your tummy in and out (your rib cage remains relatively still) or by raising and lowering your rib cage.

If the organs of the **thorax** (chest) are protected in this way, then why not those of the **abdomen** (belly)? There is a pay-off between flexibility and protection – in general, the better the protection, the less flexibility there is. To allow the body to bend and rotate above the hips, the body does not have bones surrounding the abdomen. To compensate, thick muscular walls (the proverbial 'six-pack') surround it. These muscles allow movement, but also give protection. When they are flexed, they can become quite rigid: a blow to the abdomen can be absorbed with much less damage than a blow to the head (the brain can rattle around quite a bit inside the skull). As well as needing flexibility for movement, the mammalian abdomen needs to be flexible to allow expansion as a result of eating or foetal growth.

Bone structure

The rigidity of bone is derived from its inorganic content (65–70% by mass), which is mostly calcium. This provides bone with a structure that is very strong in compression but weaker in bending (in other words, bones can withstand great pressure, but are liable to snap when bent). Without a rigid internal structure, mammals and other vertebrates would lose their shape and end up looking like rather badly filled bean bags. Animals that don't have a rigid body structure (either internally or externally) tend to be either very small, or restricted to an aquatic life form where the surrounding water can act as a support.

The long structural bones within the body, particularly those in the limbs, contain a central core of organic or living material (see below) surrounded by a rigid inorganic component. The structure of bone has similarities to that of wood, in that it consists of parallel fibres or strands running the length of the bone. Bundling drinking straws or paper tubes together can model this: the structure is strong in compression, but not so strong when you try to bend it. Healthy bones are not brittle: they tend to be quite tough, due to the gelatine and fatty tissues between the fibres providing some elasticity. The bones of young mammals, due to their rapid early growth, tend to be less rigid than adult bones, and thus more flexible and less likely to break.

Cell production

The organic or living part of the bone (apart from its blood supply system) is in the central core or **marrow**. There are two types of bone marrow cell: the yellow fat cells and the red blood-producing cells. Most of the production of blood cells (both red and white) occurs in the ribs and the pelvis. More details on mammalian blood are given on page 58.

Movement

Bones allow movement: muscles do the actual pulling, but bones are what they pull against. The bones act as levers within the body, allowing movement about a **joint** (where two or more bones are connected). There are various different forms of joint. Some do not allow any movement at all, such as those where the bones of the skull meet; hinge and 'ball and socket' joints allow the greatest degree of controlled movement (see Figure 2). Bones that meet at a

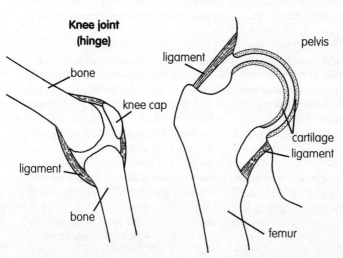

Hip joint (ball and socket)

Knee joint (hinge)

pelvis

ligament

bone

knee cap

cartilage
ligament

ligament

bone

femur

Figure 2

Figure 3

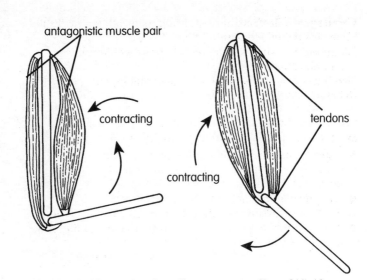

antagonistic muscle pair

contracting

contracting

tendons

joint are held together by a **ligament**: a collar of tough, fibrous material that prevents the bones from moving out of alignment, and also prevents the liquid that lubricates the joint (**synovial fluid**) from leaking away.

To increase ease of movement and reduce friction, the ends of the bones are also coated with a rubbery **cartilage**. When mammals and other animals are born, most of their skeleton is made up of cartilage rather than bone (for greater flexibility and faster growth). In old age, the cartilage between bones can wear away, allowing the bones at joints to come into direct contact and rub against each other. This process, known as **arthritis**, can result in pain and loss of mobility.

To achieve movement about a joint, **muscles** have to act. Muscles are bundles of long cells that can contract (shorten) and relax (lengthen). They are attached to the bones across a joint by very strong cords or **tendons**. Muscles are usually attached in pairs: one to pull the bone one way, and another to pull it back. When one of a pair of **antagonistic** muscles contracts and the other goes limp, the bone will move about the joint (see Figure 3).

Why you need to know these facts

Children often associate bones and the skeleton with death, because the bones only become visible when the rest of the body has decayed. Knowing about the skeleton as a part of the body will demystify it and help children to understand what functions it performs for living mammals.

Cartilage – a flexible, hard-wearing material that protects bones from damage within joints.
Ligament – tissue that connects bones together and surrounds joints.
Tendon – very strong, inelastic tissue that connects muscles to bones.

- There are 206 bones in the human body.
- A giraffe has the same number of neck bones (cervical vertebrae) as a human – but the giraffe's neck bones are longer.
- One third of the mass of a bone is water.
- 3–5% of your body weight is bone marrow.
- The gelatine in animal bones is used to make jellies, non-dairy cream and glue.

All hard bits in the body are bone.
By feeling your body, you can identify the positions of bones. Some of the hard bits may also be either tendon or cartilage. The ear and the end of the nose have a hard but semi-flexible structure. This is cartilage: a tough, rubbery substance that is shaped (feel your ears) and can be bent, but will spring back into its original shape. The hard parts of your throat and larynx are also made of cartilage.

If you flex your arm or leg into a right angle, you can feel some hard strands in the pit of your elbow or knee. These are the tendons, which attach the muscles to the bones. The most noticeable tendons are the Achilles tendons at the back of the ankles. Some fish, such as sharks, don't have any bones: their skeletons are entirely composed of cartilage.

What are bones like inside?
Bones are not the same wherever you look. They have a skin called the **periosteum**, which is where new bone grows. At the ends of a long bone (such as those in the limbs) it looks like a sponge: full of holes, but light and strong. Running down the centre of the bone is a jelly-like material called bone marrow, which is where blood cells are made. Between the marrowbone core and the outer skin is a dense, compact form of bone which is very strong. It does have some small holes in it to allow tiny blood vessels access to the bone cells.

Are all bones hard?

New-born mammals start life with many of their bones made only from cartilage. This allows them to be more flexible and grow faster. If you leave a chicken bone in a pot of vinegar for a few days, the acid in the vinegar will eat away the calcium in the bone, allowing you to bend it without it snapping.

Do your teeth count as bones?

Although teeth are made mostly from the same material as bones (calcium), they are considerably harder. They have to resist acid in the saliva, and have a very hard outer covering (enamel) so that they do not wear away too fast. Teeth are much more solid than the spongy interior of most large bones.

How long do bones go on growing?

Once bones reach adult size, they stop getting any bigger – but they never stop growing. Bones are living, not lumps of rock, so the cells have to be continually renewed. This means that if a bone is broken, it can knit back together again (rather like the skin when it is cut) and be as strong as before.

Teaching ideas

Skeletal drawings (observing, presenting)

The *Funnybones* books by Janet and Allan Ahlberg (Mammoth) may well be familiar to the children – but they do not give a very accurate view of skeletal structure. Ask the children to draw what they think their skeleton would look like, using chalk on black paper. Encourage them to feel along their limbs to identify the joints between bones. Repeat with an animal for which you can obtain a skeleton in a case. This activity is particularly interesting to use as a 'before and after' assessment activity where the children can compare their two drawings.

Bone structure (observing, modelling)

The children can make a model bone by taping together a bundle of five or six drinking straws or tightly rolled up sheets of paper. They can try to compress their bundle from each end (lengthways) and note how strong it is. Now they can try to bend the bundle – in this plane, it is relatively weak. Explain that long bones are fibrous, like the straws: they are strong in compression, but quite weak when you try to bend them.

Joint effort (observing, testing)

Ask the children to work their way around their bodies, operating one joint at a time. Can they identify how each joint moves? Is it in one plane, like the joints in the fingers – a hinge joint? Is there greater movement, as in the shoulder – a ball and socket joint?

Concept 3: Beating and breathing

Heart and lungs

Subject facts

The heart and lungs of any mammal can be found within the chest or **thoracic cavity**, protected and supported by a cage of flexible bones – the ribs. The flexibility allows for expansion and contraction, caused by the **inhalation** of air into the lungs and its **exhalation** out again. The heart is between the lungs in a central position, slightly to the left (see Figure 4).

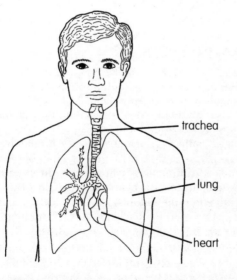

trachea

lung

heart

Figure 4

The muscle that never rests

The heart is the hardest-working muscle in the body: it is continually contracting and relaxing from before birth to the point of death. Generally speaking, the smaller the mammal, the faster the heart rate.

The mammalian heart is effectively two pumps: one side receiving blood from the body and pumping it to the lungs, the other receiving blood from the lungs and returning it to the body. The efficiency of this design is fairly amazing and, if exercised properly, nearly maintenance-free. The structure of the heart is quite simple (see Figure 5), though the number of blood vessels connecting it to the rest of the body can make it appear confusing.

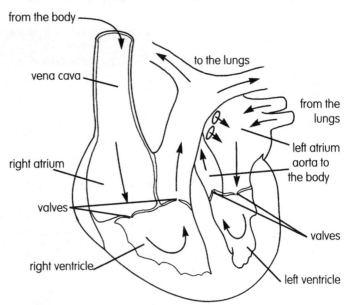

from the body

to the lungs

vena cava

from the lungs

left atrium
aorta to
the body

right atrium

valves

valves

right ventricle

left ventricle

Figure 5

Blood flows towards the heart from different parts of the body through tubes called **veins** that become increasingly large as they merge, finally entering the heart through a huge vein called the **vena cava** (on a human heart, this will be at the top on the right). The first chamber that the blood enters is a 'waiting area' called the **right atrium**. In between contractions, blood is able to flow through a one-way **valve** into the main chamber or **right ventricle**. When the heart beats, the muscle tissue surrounding it contracts, squeezing the ventricle. The blood that has flowed into it is forced out again; but it can't go out the way it came in, because the pressure on the valve leading back to the atrium has closed it – so the only way out is through a strong-walled blood vessel or **artery** to the lungs. This too has a valve leading to it, preventing blood from flowing back into the right ventricle.

As the blood passes through the lungs, an exchange of gases takes place (see page 57). From the lungs, the blood returns to the left-hand side of the heart. Here, it collects in the left ventricle before being forced out by the contraction of the heart into the main artery or **aorta**. The aorta is basically a distribution centre to which arteries leading to different parts of the body are connected. As the blood leaves the left side of the heart it is under considerable pressure, so the artery walls have to be thick and muscular. For protection, arteries tend to run deep inside the body.

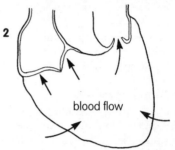

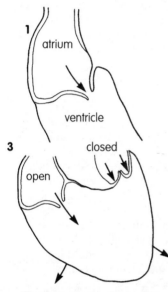

1. Ventricle expands; outside pressure of blood forces it through valve into ventricle.
2. Ventricle contracts; pressure of blood inside closes valve leading back to atrium and opens valve leading to arteries.
3. Muscles relax; blood flows from atrium.

Figure 6

The keys to the flow of blood through the heart are the **valves** (see Figure 6). Also, to ensure that blood continues to flow in the right direction as it returns to the heart, all of the larger veins have valves along their length to prevent 'backflow'. You can demonstrate this on yourself; on the underside of your wrist, you will probably be able to make out a series of blue lines. If you press down on one of these and draw your finger slowly up your arm, following the line, you will probably see the line disappear as the blood is pressed out of it. When you release your grip, the line will reappear.

Fortunately, all of the actions of the heart are completely automatic: no effort or thinking is required! The heartbeat is controlled by the **autonomic nervous system** (see Concept 5, page 68), which regulates processes within the body that are not under conscious control. The body produces natural stimulants to increase blood flow when necessary (for example, during exercise). The sounds that the heart makes as it beats are caused by valves closing: in the 'lub-dub' sound, the 'lub' is the closing of the valves between the atria and the ventricles; the sharper-sounding 'dub' is the snapping shut of the valves leading to the arteries.

Because of this repeated squeezing action, blood travels around the body in a series of squirts. This uneven flow or **pulse** of blood can be felt at various places around the body where an artery is close to a hard body part (bone, cartilage or tendon), making it vibrate. The best places to experience these pulses on yourself are on the inside of the wrist (just behind the thumb) and on the neck (at the inner sides just under the jaw). The normal 'at rest' adult heart rate is 70–80 beats per minute.

Heart problems

There are three main ways in which the heart can be damaged and function less well. The first, a defect often spotted at birth, is a 'hole in the heart'. This does not mean that there is a hole in the external wall of the heart, allowing blood to leak out into the thoracic cavity: if this were the problem, it is unlikely that a live birth would be possible. The 'hole' is a leak between the two ventricles, which allows oxygen-poor blood (see page 58) to cross over and be pumped back around the body a second time, or allows oxygen-rich blood to take a second trip through the lungs. Any mammal suffering from this condition is unlikely to be able to be as fast or as strong, or have as much endurance, as others of the species.

The heart valves of ageing mammals can also become less efficient and allow blood to flow backwards, so that the heart has to do more work to move the blood.

Humans tend to be the only mammals with heart problems that are self-inflicted through poor or inappropriate diet (see Chapter 4, page 87). If we eat too much animal fat and take insufficient exercise, the inner surfaces of our blood vessels can become coated with fatty plaque. This reduces the bore (internal width) of the vessels and so restricts the flow of blood, leading to a build-up of pressure. This high blood pressure can strain the heart muscles, causing them to 'flutter' rather than contract strongly – a 'heart attack'. When this happens, there are two medical options: to insert a new blood vessel that can 'bypass' the blocked parts; or to insert and inflate a balloon in the restricted section to compress the plaque against the vessel walls, so that blood flow can increase once the balloon has been removed.

Breathing

The mammalian **lungs** are a very effective way of extracting oxygen from air. The tissue that they are made from appears very spongy, and is full of very small chambers or sacs called **alveoli**. Air enters the lungs from the **trachea** or breathing tube, and passes through **bronchial tubes** that subdivide into smaller and smaller tubes, eventually terminating in bunches of alveoli (see Figure 7). The walls of these tiny sacs are very thin – only a couple of cells – and are lined with a slimy **mucus** into which gases can dissolve. The bunches of alveoli are surrounded by small, thin-walled blood vessels called **capillaries**, which transport blood to and from the lungs.

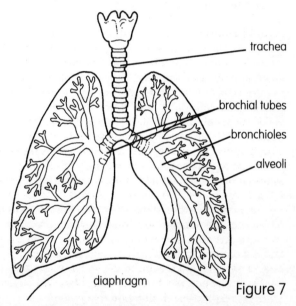

trachea

brochial tubes

bronchioles

alveoli

diaphragm

Figure 7

The design of the lungs provides a very large surface area within a limited volume. Surface area is important, because the surface is where the exchange of gases takes place. Oxygen contained within the air diffuses into the red blood cells, and the carbon dioxide carried by the red blood cells diffuses back into the air to complete the exchange.

The act of breathing in is caused by the **diaphragm** (a sheet of muscle that separates the thorax from the abdomen) tightening and pulling down. Something has to fill the extra space that has been made in the thorax, so air is drawn into the lungs, causing them to expand. As the diaphragm relaxes it once more arches up, compressing the lungs and causing them to expel air. If you hold yourself around your chest, you can feel how your chest expands as you breathe – but this is not the only method of breathing! 'Tummy breathing' allows the lungs to inflate with the chest moving as little as possible: you move your abdominal organs out of the way instead. By combining both methods – sticking your chest and tummy out – you can really fill your lungs (which is very helpful if you are singing or playing a trumpet).

Although the act of breathing is to some extent an automatic response, similar to your heartbeat, it is possible to exert much more control over it. You can physically make yourself stop breathing for a minute or so, before the automatic responses take over. You breathe in as an automatic response to a build-up of carbon dioxide. In a relaxed, resting state you do not need a great deal of oxygen, so your breathing is shallow and the exchange of gases is quite small in proportion to the capacity of your lungs. Every so often the carbon dioxide builds up to such an extent that a near-complete change of air in the lungs is required: this results in a sigh or a yawn, which amounts to a single deep breath. A good deep breath of 'fresh air' makes you feel more alert, mainly because an over-saturation of carbon dioxide makes you feel drowsy. During mouth-to-mouth artificial respiration, it is as much the high proportion of carbon dioxide being breathed into the lungs as the inflation of the lungs that restarts the breathing reflex.

The oxygen/carbon dioxide exchange that takes place in the alveoli is not a complete one. During normal breathing, only a quarter of the available oxygen breathed in diffuses into the blood supply; so where a normal oxygen concentration of 20% is breathed in, the concentration in the air on the way out is still usually about 16% – otherwise, artificial respiration couldn't do much good!

Blood and respiration

Mammalian blood has four main components:
- **white cells** – these come in a variety of forms, and attack infections within the blood
- **platelets** – small bits of cells that form a clot or scab when a blood vessel is damaged (especially when they are exposed to air)
- **plasma** – the yellowish liquid, about 90% water, that carries the blood cells and other material around the body
- **red cells** – these transport gases for respiration; they contain the pigment **haemoglobin**, which gives the blood its red colour.

In the lungs, oxygen diffuses into the red blood cells. Once the oxygen has been delivered to where it is needed (see Concept 6, page 71), the red blood cells carry the waste carbon dioxide back to the lungs.

Respiration and energy

The purpose of respiration is to deliver energy in a usable form to all parts of the body. The blood delivers carbohydrate (sugar) and oxygen to the body tissues, where they are combined to release energy. This process is known as **aerobic respiration**. Its main waste product, carbon dioxide, is taken back to the lungs by the blood. Other waste products of body chemistry, such as urea, are filtered out as the blood passes through the kidneys.

There are times, usually during strenuous exercise, when aerobic respiration cannot supply as much energy as the most active muscles need. At such times, energy release can take place without oxygen for short periods (**anaerobic respiration**). The waste product of this process, **lactic acid**, is toxic: it causes muscle fatigue. To get rid of it, oxygen has to be used up; so there is an 'oxygen debt' to be paid back, causing the period of puffing and panting and increased heart rate that follows sudden exercise. During sustained exercise, the oxygen debt may be paid back – resulting in a new surge of aerobic energy (the 'second wind').

The mammalian heart-lungs system is a very effective means of distributing the energy obtained from food to different parts of the body and making use of it. Sugars obtained from food are combined with oxygen to release energy that allows mammals to perform their various functions. The waste products of this process are then recycled or expelled. Understanding these processes will allow children to appreciate the need to maintain their own bodies (see Chapter 4, page 85) and instil a sense of wonder at the complexities of nature.

Why you need to know these facts

Veins – the tubes carrying blood towards the heart.
Arteries – the tubes carrying blood away from the heart.
Ventricles – the large, muscular chambers of the heart.
Atria (plural of **atrium**) – the smaller heart chambers through which the blood passes to reach the ventricles.
Heart – the muscle that pumps the blood around the body.
Valves – flaps of muscle that are positioned to prevent the reverse flow of blood.

Vocabulary

Pulse – the rhythmic flow of blood along the arteries.
Capillaries – very fine (small-bore) blood vessels.
Red blood cells – cells that carry oxygen and carbon dioxide in the bloodstream.
Lungs – the organs that extract oxygen from the air.
Diaphragm – a muscle sheet that allows air to be drawn into the lungs.
Aerobic respiration – the release of energy in body tissues, using oxygen.
Anaerobic respiration – the short-term release of energy without the use of oxygen, leading to a build-up of lactic acid.

Amazing facts

● The average human heart beats 2.5 billion times in its life. This is roughly the same number of heartbeats that a mouse living to the ripe old age of seven years will manage (at about 500 beats per minute.)
● Whales have been known to hold their breath for over two hours while diving for food.
● The average lung capacity of an adult human is 5–6 litres.
● A whale heart has been known to weigh almost 700kg. A human heart weighs less than 1kg, and is about the size of a fist.
● A rat will take 100–200 breaths per minute, while a horse or an elephant will take only five. Humans take 16–20 breaths per minute – that's 23 000 per day, or enough air to fill a room 2.5m³.
● Humans make new red blood cells at a rate of 2 million per second. Human blood contains 500 red cells for every white cell.
● Air rushes out of your nose at 160km/h when you sneeze – about the speed of a hurricane.

Common misconceptions

Mammals breathe in oxygen and breathe out carbon dioxide.
This is too great a simplification. The air that we breathe in will have a greater oxygen content and a smaller carbon dioxide content than the air we breathe out. Lungs do not extract all of the oxygen content from the air in each breath and replace it entirely with carbon dioxide.

You yawn when you are tired.
You are likely to yawn or sigh when the carbon dioxide content of the air in your lungs reaches a point where your

body attempts to force a complete refill of the lungs. This is more likely to happen when you have been fairly inactive for a while, and have been breathing rather shallowly – which may be the case if you are tired, but also if you are trying to keep still or if there is too much carbon dioxide in the air around you.

What are hiccups?
These short, sharp breaths occur when the diaphragm, which controls the expansion and contraction of the lungs, goes into a spasm and makes regular jerky movements. This can be brought on by a temporary loss of breath. It usually wears off after a couple of minutes.

If somebody's heart stops in a TV hospital drama, they give them an electric shock. Why?
All muscles work – tense and then relax – because of very small electrical impulses sent to them through nerves (see Concept 5). The electric shock given to patients by a **defibrillator** makes the heart muscles tense up; when they relax, the body's own automatic system may be able to start working again. Some people with heart problems are fitted with a **pacemaker**, which gives a regular small electric shock to the heart to make it beat regularly.

Teaching ideas

To avoid distressing animals, most activities relating to heart rates and breathing are best carried out by the children on themselves – under controlled conditions where any medical problems are known and allowed for. Emphasize that the children should never subject animals to abnormal or stressful conditions. Taking their own pet dog out for a normal 'run on the common' and observing its respiration and heart rates before and after exercise would be acceptable. Making a hamster run for five minutes in a wheel and then passing it around a group, so they can feel its heart rate, would **not** be!

Obtaining mammal hearts and lungs from a butcher to cut up and observe in close detail is problematic in terms of hygiene, ethics and practical issues; the sensibilities of vegans or vegetarians must be taken into consideration. Besides, the dangers of cutting tools and the sheer messiness of such an activity in the average primary classroom make it inappropriate in almost all cases. Videos and computer-based simulations offer an appropriate alternative to first-hand sources.

Modelling the heart (explaining, modelling)

If we simplify the heart to a two-chamber model (ventricles only), its main actions can be modelled by four children, with the rest of the class acting as the 'blood'. Each ventricle is made up of two children, facing each other with their arms outstretched and touching. Another child (as some blood) 'flows' from the 'body' between two hands into the area contained within the arms, then is pushed by the arms to make him or her 'flow' through the other pair of hands (towards the 'lungs'). The arms then reach back to collect the next child and push him or her through. Another pair of children act as the other chamber, pumping the 'blood' that returns from the 'lungs' back into the 'body'.

Lung capacity (testing, measuring)

You will need a large plastic sweet jar, a large bowl of water (bigger than the sweet jar) and a length of PVC tubing. Ask the children to measure both their lung capacity and their normal respiration flow, as follows:
1. Calibrate the jar by pouring in water 50ml or 100ml at a time and marking each level on the side.
2. Now fill the jar completely with water (no air at all) and invert it in the bowl of water. Insert the tube into the jar, take a very deep breath and blow into the tube. The amount of air in the jar is your lung capacity.
3. A normal breath into the tube will show you how much air is normally used: only a small proportion of the lungs' total capacity.

Journey in the blood (explaining, hypothesizing)

The children can describe the cycle of a red blood cell or an oxygen particle within the mammalian respiration cycle. They can use drawings, an imaginative story, a cartoon strip or a drama, as they prefer (and according to their abilities).

Concept 4: The digestive system

Subject facts

Figure 8 shows a simplified diagram of the human digestive system. Other mammals have similar systems, though there may be some differences due to the types of food that they eat – some types of food take a lot more digesting than others, so some mammals are adapted accordingly.

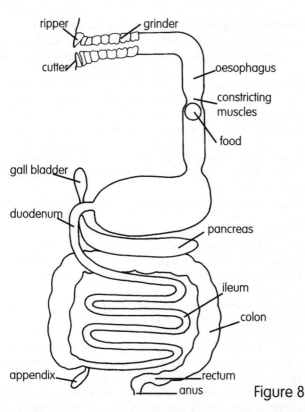

ripper

grinder

cutter

oesophagus

constricting muscles

food

gall bladder

duodenum

pancreas

ileum

colon

appendix

rectum

anus

Figure 8

The mouth

The mouth is where the **digestion** (breaking down) of food begins. In mammals, two distinct digestive processes take place in the mouth. The first is the use of teeth to break food down physically into smaller pieces (whereas many reptiles and birds, particularly carnivorous ones, swallow food whole). Most teeth can be described as cutters (**incisors**), rippers (**canines**) or grinders (**molars**). Carnivores will usually have rippers: pointed fang-like teeth for ripping flesh off the bone. Herbivores will have cutters at the front and grinders at the back. Omnivores (such as humans and bears) will have a full mix. The food is cut into manageable pieces by the front cutting teeth; then the tongue transfers it to the back of the mouth, where it is ground up and mixed with saliva into a paste before being swallowed.

The other digestive process going on in the mouth involves **saliva**. This mildly acidic, lubricating liquid begins to break down starch-based foods (see page 88) into sugars, which can be digested more easily. Saliva also adds moisture to the food, allowing it to be swallowed.

Down the hatch...

It has probably not escaped your notice that the mouth can be used for both food and air. There are two tubes leading out of the back of the mouth: the **trachea** and the **oesophagus**. The action of swallowing closes the trachea (the air passage) and opens the oesophagus (which leads to the stomach). The oesophagus is ringed with muscles that constrict above the food ball, forcing it downwards – a process known as **peristalsis**. Gravity also helps the food to descend: eating while upside down is difficult!

In some mammals, known as **ruminants** (such as the cow), these muscles also work in reverse: they bring the food back up for a second chew. These mammals have more than one stomach chamber, because the food they live on requires a lot of work to digest: they often obtain most of their energy from plant fibre or **cellulose** (for example, in grass), which requires a lot of enzyme action before digestion can be completed.

Into the stomach...

The **stomach** is a holding bay for further digestion, allowing the digested food to be released into the **duodenum** (the top end of the **small intestine**) in a regulated way. In the stomach, the food is sprayed with **hydrochloric acid**. This tenderizes the food and kills most of the germs on it, preparing it for the **digestive enzymes** (complex biological molecules that stimulate chemical changes) to get to work on. The mucus coating of the stomach lining normally prevents the stomach lining from being attacked by the acid. (If this protection breaks down, stomach ulcers will develop.) At this point, an enzyme called **pepsin** begins to break protein down into **amino acids,** and other enzymes begin to break down other food types. Water and some simple sugars are absorbed into the body through the stomach lining.

A long and winding road...

The **small intestine** (so called because of the diameter of the tube, not the length) is called the **duodenum** where it leaves the stomach and the **ileum** further down. On leaving the stomach the food, which is now a thick, soupy liquid known as **chyme**, is sprayed with **bile**. Bile is a liquid made in the liver and stored in the gall bladder; it breaks down fats into tiny droplets, giving them a larger surface area for the enzymes to act on. Bile also neutralizes the stomach acids, allowing the enzymes to work more effectively. These enzymes are released into the duodenum from the

pancreas, and include **lipase** (digests fat into fatty acids), **carbohydrase** (digests starch into glucose) and **protease** (completes the digestion of proteins).

The remaining length of the small intestine, the ileum, follows up digestion with **absorption**. The food, reduced to very simple forms as a result of the enzyme action, can now be absorbed into the blood supply through the blood capillaries in the lining of the ileum.

And finally, down the waste chute...
The **colon** (or **large intestine**) collects all of the undigested food, most of which will be indigestible. This slurry is reduced to a more solid state by the extraction of most of the moisture content, which helps to prevent dehydration. A notable addition at this stage is a vast quantity of dead red blood cells. Indeed, almost a third of the total mass of faeces produced is used red blood cells – giving the waste its unmistakeable colour.

The chemical factory
Once the food has been absorbed into the blood, most of it is transported to the **liver** for further processing. The liver performs many essential functions. From the digested food, it manufactures proteins (including anti-infection and clotting agents) and produces oxygen- and fat-carrying compounds. It produces bile (see above), which is stored next to it in the **gall bladder.** It is also able to counter the effects of some poisons by filtering them from the bloodstream, then neutralizing and excreting them. The human liver is positioned just under the diaphragm, on the right hand side of the body.

Children are fascinated to discover what happens to food once it has been swallowed, and how it can be turned into something that is useful to mammals (in terms of growth or movement). The chemical processes that form the basis of digestion are quite detailed; but simplified models can help the children to begin to understand them.

Why you need to know these facts

Digestion – the process of breaking food down into simple chemicals for absorption by the body.
Mouth – where food is physically broken down into smaller pieces and moisture is added.
Incisors – cutting teeth.
Canines – ripping teeth.

Vocabulary

Molars – grinding teeth.

Saliva – a lubricating digestive juice produced in the mouth.

Stomach – a rounded vessel in the body where acidic digestive juices are added to the food to reduce it to a 'thick soup' called chyme.

Duodenum – the upper part of the small intestine, where further enzymes and bile are added to the chyme to break down the more complex foods.

Ileum – the lower end of the small intestine where the digested food is absorbed into the body via the blood supply.

Colon – the large intestine, where the undigested food has moisture removed from it and dead red blood cells are added prior to excretion.

Amazing facts

● Food takes between 10 and 20 hours to pass through the human digestive tract, spending up to three hours in the stomach alone.

● The adult human intestine is up to 8m long.

● Ruminants are able to snatch a lot of food quickly and then 'eat' it properly later. This is very useful if you are likely to be attacked by a predator at any moment! Of the ruminants, camels and llamas have three stomachs; sheep, cattle and goats have four.

● The digestive system of the giant panda is based on digesting meat rather than the bamboo that is its staple diet. This helps to explain why it is in danger of becoming extinct: it is too reliant on a poor source of nutrition – and too specialized to go back to eating meat.

● The liver can lose up to 75% of its tissue (to disease or surgery) and still keep working. This is why transplants usually only involve a section of the donor's liver.

Common misconceptions

All food is digested in the stomach.
Simpler foods, such as sugars, are digested and absorbed in the stomach; but most foods will travel on into the small intestine for further digestion before being absorbed into the blood.

Questions

What happens when you are sick?
Vomiting is the result of the body reacting to impulses from the brain's 'vomit centre' (yes, there really is one!). This centre may receive signals from the stomach (that it is overloaded, or contains something disagreeable or

poisonous), from the inner ear (the balance centre, which is disturbed in motion sickness), or from sense organs (particularly taste and smell). Whatever the stimulus that provokes it, the vomiting reflex is essentially the same: the diaphragm presses down on the stomach at the same time that the valve between the stomach and the oesophagus relaxes, allowing the stomach contents to be pushed upwards. The sour taste of vomit is due to the gastric juices from the stomach – but the presence of diced carrot is still a scientific mystery!

Why do you burp?
Burping (or belching) is caused by the release of gas trapped in the stomach. This gas may be air swallowed while eating too quickly, carbon dioxide from fizzy drinks or gases released as a result of digestion. Any gases released at the other end tend to be the result of the digestive processes acting on a high-fibre diet.

As with the heart and lungs, I would not recommend obtaining a mammalian digestive tract from a butcher for inspection or dissection! Work on this topic is best done using reference materials.

Teeth and diet (observing, comparing)
Looking at pictures of the skulls of mammals (or even of faces showing teeth) will allow the children to make deductions about the kind of diet each animal lives on. (Also see Chapter 7, page 150.) They can check their deductions by referring to books on pets, wildlife videos and CD-ROM nature encyclopaedias.

Journey in the gut (explaining, describing)
Ask the children to take on the role of a piece of food and to describe their journey as they travel through the digestive tract. This could be presented as a story, a newspaper report, a cartoon strip, a series of pictures or a piece of drama. The BBC series *The Human Body* provides some excellent images as a stimulus.

Digestive navigation (exploring, observing)
The children can work in small groups to navigate themselves through the digestive system, using software such as *The Magic School Bus (Human Body)* from Microsoft. They could then be encouraged to write a diary entry or news report on their journey.

Components of the nervous system

The mammalian nervous system has two interconnecting parts: the central nervous system and the peripheral nervous system.

The **central nervous system** (the brain and spinal cord) processes and co-ordinates all the information coming in from sense organs and the outgoing commands to muscles. The **brain** is a mass of nervous tissue in which complex functions such as memory, intelligence, learning and emotion occur. The **spinal cord** is a long nerve that connects the brain to the rest of the body.

The **peripheral nervous system** is all of the nervous tissue outside the brain and the spinal cord. It is responsible for sending information to, and receiving it from, the rest of the body. Instructions to move, which are sent out through the **motor nerves**, can either be **voluntary** (as when moving muscles to stand up) or **involuntary** (as when muscles control the flow of food in the digestive system). The part of the nervous system that controls involuntary movements is also known as **autonomic**.

The autonomic nervous system is further divided into the **sympathetic** and **parasympathetic** nervous systems. The first of these produces the 'fight or flight' response: it increases alertness and stimulates the body, preparing it for danger. The second produces the 'rest and repose' response: it conserves energy for normal bodily functions such as digestion.

Transmission and communication

A **nerve cell** or **neuron** receives and passes on information in the form of electrical pulses. Figure 9 shows how a **sensory neuron** works. Small protrusions from the cell, known as **dendrites**, receive stimulation from a sense organ (see Concept 7, page 74) or another neuron. When stimulated, the neuron undergoes a slight change in its chemical content, resulting in the production of a small electrical impulse. This impulse travels along the **axon**, a sort of long tail that can be up to 1m long. When it reaches the end of the axon, chemical **transmitters** are released which travel across a gap, called a **synapse**, to the dendrite of the next neuron – and so the signal passes on to the appropriate section of the brain for processing. **Motor neurons**, which convey instructions from the brain to muscles or other organs, have a slightly different structure, but they work in a similar way.

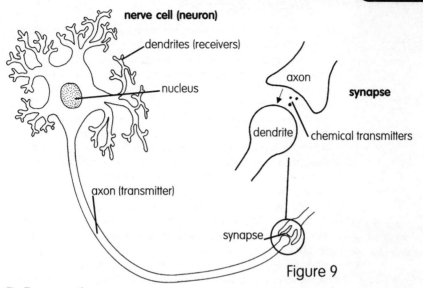

nerve cell (neuron)

dendrites (receivers)

nucleus

axon

synapse

dendrite

chemical transmitters

axon (transmitter)

synapse

Figure 9

Reflex reactions

Sometimes a stimulus is such that the information doesn't
even need to get to the brain before action is taken. The
difference between 'very warm' and 'hot' may be marginal –
but reactions to it will be significantly different. If a very
warm object is picked up, the brain will make a conscious
decision to put it down before the heat causes damage. With
a hot object, the signals about the heat only get as far as the
spinal cord before messages are sent to the muscles to drop
the object and move away from it. A message will also be
sent to the brain to let it know what has happened. **Reflex
reactions** of this kind – very fast and completely automatic –
have obvious survival value.

Links to learning

Almost as rapid as reflex reactions are the 'learned
responses' that we make to familiar stimuli – for example, a
driver stopping at a red light. This phenomenon can be
linked to issues surrounding early learning. When a new
skill is being learned, considerable effort and concentration
is needed. Writing needs initially to be thought about and
focused on – but once the skill has been learned, it can be
carried out 'automatically'. I no linger have to thonk where
partuculear lerrets are on the keyboard of my computer
(except when I start to think about it, and then I **really** have
to think about it). I just think of a word, my fingers move
and the word appears on the screen – but such a response
takes time and practice to become embedded.

Why you need to know these facts

Many of our everyday movements and reactions appear to be quite automatic. Some of them, such as the heartbeat, are truly automatic. Even when you make a conscious decision to do something, for example to scratch behind your left ear with your left index finger, an incredibly complex series of events has to take place to ensure that the correct muscles are operated in the correct order with the correct intensity until the response comes from the skin that the itch has been scratched. Beginning to appreciate this greatly undervalued aspect of our body control systems is an important factor in developing children's understanding of their own worth.

Vocabulary

Reflex – an involuntary reaction in response to a particular stimulus.
Involuntary – nervous messages that are sent automatically (for example, to control the heartbeat).
Voluntary – nervous messages involving conscious actions such as walking.
Brain – the organ that receives and analyzes sensory input, and controls actions.
Spinal cord – a long nerve that is the main conduit for messages and signals to and from the brain.

Amazing facts

● Some mammals have deeply embedded responses to certain 'danger signals', such as the smell of a lion or the sound of a wolf.
● Messages pass along nerve cells (neurons) at up to 400km/h.

Questions

Why do you jump when you hear a sudden, loud noise?
The sound is received by the ear, like any other sound – but the high volume overloads the nerves that send the impulses to the brain, causing a message to be sent directly to the co-ordinating section of the spinal cord, which sends messages to muscles telling them to move. So before the brain has even registered the sound, the body is beginning to move in preparation for running away. It only works for sudden sounds, because the reflex reaction wears off if the sound continues. Continuous loud noises can be 'blacked out' by the brain, and pushed in to the background because the body adjusts to them.

Why do doctors test your reflexes?
(They usually do this by tapping your knee.) This is a simple way to test the efficiency of the nerve signals travelling along the spinal cord.

Knee-jerk reaction (testing, observing)

Ask a child to sit cross-legged on a chair (with one knee over another). Gently tap just under the knee with the edge of a ruler – the leg should jerk upwards. **Safety note: all taps MUST be applied gently!** This happens because the tendon below the knee has been dented and so lengthened where it was hit. The body's automatic response is to keep the leg in position by keeping the tendon the same length. In this case, it is 'fooled' into shortening the tendon and bringing the leg up. Now try comparing the speed of the reflex with that of the response to the command 'Lift'. When the message has to go via the brain, which has to understand the message and act on it, the reaction will take longer.

Ruler drop (testing, observing)

Hold the bottom end of a 30cm ruler just above the open finger and thumb grasp of a child. Release the ruler. How far does the ruler drop before it is grasped? Does the reaction get faster with practice? Is the reaction faster if the stimulus (of the ruler being released) is visual, aural or tactile – that is, if you watch the ruler, hear someone say 'Now!' (while your eyes are closed) or feel the ruler drop?

Concept 6: Muscle reactions

Types of muscle tissue

There are three types of muscle in the mammalian body:
● **Smooth muscles** are what give the internal organs, skin and blood vessels their shape and tone. They are normally very elastic, though in old age they become more brittle and begin to lose their elasticity.
● **Cardiac muscles** are very special muscles that are only found in the heart. They seem to have a lattice of fibres, rather than bunches of parallel strands. Scientists are still trying to discover exactly how they work.

● **Skeletal muscles** are the ones that can be flexed to cause movement. Because they are easier to investigate than the other types, they are the focus of this section.

Muscle structure

Skeletal muscle tissue consists of long, fibrous muscle cells held together in bundles. Each muscle **fibre** is divided into many smaller **filaments** that fit together in a similar way to the fingers of two hands (see Figure 10). When relaxed, these filaments are quite well separated; but when stimulated, they slide closer together and bunch up, which shortens the effective length of the fibre. This causes the whole muscle to contract, resulting in a movement.

There are two forms of this type of muscle fibre: 'slow' and 'fast-twitch' fibres. **Slow fibres** are lighter in colour and have greater endurance; **fast-twitch fibres** are darker and react faster to stimuli, giving more immediate power. Most

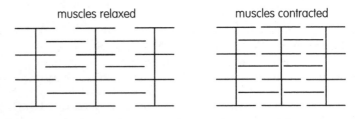

muscles relaxed   muscles contracted

Figure 10

skeletal muscles are made of a mixture of both types, but some will have more of one type than the other. Cheetahs have a lot of fast-twitch fibres in their muscles: they can sprint very fast, but not for long. Antelopes have more slow fibres: they can run quite fast for long periods of time. Olympic sprinters and long-distance runners probably have different proportions of each type of muscle.

Energy release

When skeletal muscles are used, they require significant amounts of energy. The blood system delivers glucose and oxygen to the muscles. Under normal, relatively restful conditions, enough oxygen is delivered to combine with the glucose to release sufficient quantities of energy for the muscles to work (**aerobic** respiration). In times of high energy requirements, such as running, more energy is needed – so breathing becomes deeper and faster, and the heart rate increases to deliver more oxygen to the muscles.

If more energy is needed than there is oxygen to convert, **anaerobic** respiration takes place. This is less efficient, and leads to the build-up of a waste product called **lactic acid**, which causes muscle fatigue. Fitness is often judged by recovery time: how long it takes to replace the 'oxygen debt' (see Concept 3, page 53).

Some of the energy released in skeletal muscles is not converted into movement, but released as heat. This is why running warms us up. It is also why we shiver when we are cold: the rapid muscle movements generate heat.

Making movements
All of these contracting and relaxing skeletal muscles are attached to bones across joints, resulting in a fairly effective levering system. Almost all muscles act in **antagonistic pairs**, so that once a bone is moved, it can be moved back (see Concept 2, page 47).

When children become aware that muscles are where most energy use in the body takes place, they can begin to understand the links between diet, fitness and exercise. In this way, understanding the role of the muscles leads to a deeper understanding of both respiration and digestion.

Why you need to know these facts

Muscle – fibrous tissue capable of contracting and combining glucose with oxygen to release energy.
Antagonistic pair – two muscles attached to bones such that they can cause a movement and its reverse movement.

Vocabulary

● The human body has over 650 muscles, some of which we never use and have allowed to become weak (such as the ear-waggling muscles that everyone has).
● Almost all of the meat that we eat is muscle tissue.
● The biggest muscles in your body are in your buttocks: the *gluteus maximus* muscles.

Amazing facts

Stronger people have more muscles.
No, not more muscles: just more highly developed muscles. Exercising a particular muscle makes the body devote more tissue-building activity to that area, and so makes the muscle grow.

Antagonistic muscle pairs (observing, modelling)

Ask the children to place a hand, palm up, under a desk and push up until they can feel pressure. They should note how the muscle at the front of their upper arm (the biceps) is stiff and the muscle at the back (the triceps) is flaccid. Now ask them to place one hand on top of the desk and push down – the biceps will now be flaccid and the triceps rigid. The biceps flex to push up, the triceps to push down.

Feeling muscle movement (observing)

Ask the children to place their fingers against their head, just above the ears, then clench their teeth. They will be able to feel their jaw muscles become tense: these muscles are attached high up on the skull to allow for maximum flexibility of movement.

Concept 7: Sensing the environment

Subject facts

The senses

Generally, it is believed that there are five senses – but this is not strictly true. Sight, smell, sound, taste and touch are the accepted five (although taste and smell are quite closely linked). But touch is not really just one sense: it is linked to the sense of acceleration (balance), the sense of direction and a few other, more unusual senses that particular animals exhibit. The ability of pigeons to sense changes in the local magnetic field is now being used for early warning of earthquakes. These are all ways in which it is possible to be aware of the local environment, so they are, strictly speaking, senses.

Vision

The mammalian eye (see Figure 11) is roughly spherical in shape, with a tough outer coating and a liquid-filled centre to prevent it from collapsing. Light enters the eye through a clear, scratch-resistant membrane called the **cornea**. Directly behind that is a cavity filled with liquid, called the **aqueous humour**. Within this is a coloured membrane, the **iris**, which can expand or contract to let more or less light into the eye. The black circular gap made by the iris is known as the **pupil**; in some nocturnal mammals, it can be as big as the cornea. The pupil is the entrance to the **optic lens**, which is made of clear fibrous tissue that is able to expand and contract to make the lens thicker or thinner, thus changing its focal length. This allows the eye to focus voluntarily on near or far-away objects.

Most of the eye is filled with a viscous liquid called the **vitreous humour**, through which the light travels on its way to the retina. The **retina** is the lining of the back of the eye, composed of light-sensitive cells. Most mammals have two types of light-sensitive cell: rods and cones. The **cones**, which are sensitive to red, blue or green light, are used only in bright conditions and register the intensity of light in a particular colour. The **rods** are effective even in very dim conditions, and are only capable of identifying motion – which is why you cannot see colours in poor light. The information received by these cells is transmitted to the optical centre of the brain through the **optic nerve**.

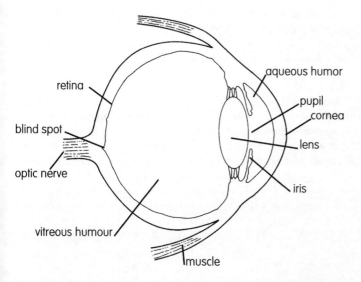

Figure 11

So, what are the eyes capable of? The mammalian eye has quite a complex design: it can be adjusted for distance, brightness, colour and direction. However, the eye itself only registers the intensity of a particular colour of light and whereabouts on the retina it fell – the rest is accomplished in the brain. The brain puts all of the coloured dots together, adjusts the lens to ensure that the resulting picture is in focus, and adjusts the iris to ensure that sufficient light is being allowed in. An impressive bit of computing – but that's not all! As the cones are only capable of registering one of three colours (red, blue or green), all of the other colours and shades that you see are literally figments of your imagination. Your brain makes up what we see as orange by extrapolating from the intensities of red and green light (and the absence of blue) in the field of vision. Also, the brain has the knack of 'turning colours down' if it decides that there is too much of one colour hitting a particular patch on the retina (see Teaching ideas below).

Although most mammals have similar eye structures, the ability of different mammals to see varies. Some moles are all but blind. Galagos (bush babies) are nocturnal and have very large eyes to collect as much light as possible. Cattle have very few cone cells, and thus are incapable of seeing any colour (so bulls cannot 'see red' at all).

The position of the eyes on the skull is important. Many herbivorous mammals, such as rabbits, have eyes on either side of their head, allowing a very wide field of vision to help them avoid predators. Predatory mammals, such as cats and dogs, have a greater need for good 3-D vision in front of them, so their eyes are on the front of the head with a large degree of overlap (see Figure 12).

Hearing

Hearing is the ability to sense **vibrations** (small oscillating movements). Not all mammals have ears, but they are all capable of hearing. Dolphins, for example, need to have a streamlined body shape, and protruding ears would get in the way; so they hear through their lower jawbone rather

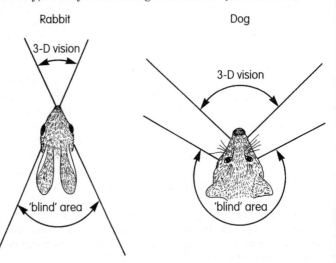

Rabbit

Dog

3-D vision

3-D vision

'blind' area

'blind' area

Figure 12

than an outer ear. However, most mammals have a three-part ear system: the inner, middle and outer ear (see Figure 13). The **outer ear** (or **pinna**) collects the sound vibrations and directs them to the **middle ear**, where three small bones transmit them to the **inner ear** (or **cochlea**). This is a liquid-filled, rolled-up cone like the shell of a snail, covered on the inside by small hairs. These hairs are the actual sound sensors, and are connected directly to the brain via the **auditory nerve**. The hairs further up the cone are sensitive to higher frequencies of sound.

Having ears placed on either side of the head means that most mammals have very effective directional hearing. Some mammals, such as bats and whales, use **echolocation** as a means of sensing objects around them: they send out 'vocalized clicks' and listen for echoes off hard objects.

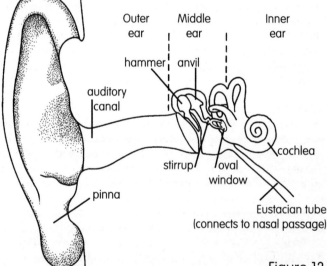

Figure 13

Whereas eyes are only capable of registering three different frequencies of light, ears are capable of detecting and distinguishing between many different frequencies of sound.

The ear also contains the **balance** organ, which senses changes in position or movement. Within the inner ear, three liquid-filled **semi-circular canals** at right angles to each other register changes in the direction and rate of movement. The liquid in them 'sloshes around' as the animal changes speed, direction, or orientation relative to gravity; sensory hairs stimulated by the liquid transmit this information to the brain.

Smell

Smell is perhaps the least well understood of the five main senses. It is closely linked to taste, and one often helps to reinforce the other. The organs of smell are very small hair-like sensors high up in the nasal cavity. When stimulated, they transmit information to the brain via the **olfactory nerves**. There are three primary colours of light to which mammalian eyes are sensitive, four primary tastes, and seven primary odours. Each different smell has a particular combination of these seven odours, and a different type of olfactory nerve registers each odour.

What scientists think happens (it is still poorly understood) is that the chemical pattern that represents each of these odours either sets off a chemical reaction in the olfactory nerve or locks onto the nerve ending (like a piece of a jigsaw). Either way, a nerve impulse is sent to the brain to register that odour. The brain then puts all of these nerve impulses together to make up an impression of a smell. Over-exposure to a particular smell will reduce the sensitivity of particular receptors, so that the smell seems to go away (for example, smokers may be unaware that they smell of smoke).

Taste

The four primary tastes are the same for all mammals, though the degree of sensitivity varies according to species, age and gender (human females have more taste buds than males). The receptors are the **taste buds**: small bumps along the tongue and at the back of the mouth near the roof. On the human tongue, the taste buds are bunched together in particular areas. **Sweet** receptors are on the tip of the tongue, **salt** and **sour** on the sides and **bitter** at the back.

Taste sensitivity varies according to temperature, time of day and a range of other variables, all of which affect the efficiency of the 9000 or so taste buds on the human tongue. It is far from being the most exact of senses. Most tastes are predominantly smells: when the olfactory sensors are not working well because your nose is blocked, you will find it much more difficult to 'taste' food.

Touch

Touch is an unusual sense, in that the sensing organ (the skin) covers the body surface entirely. It is really four distinct senses: contact, temperature, pressure and pain.

Specific receptors in the skin register **contact** with other substances. They can be used to detect the texture of a surface: rough, smooth, sticky and so on. These receptors are bunched together where they will be most effective – for example, human fingertips, the end of an elephant's trunk, the whiskers of a cat and so on.

The skin also has receptors that register **temperature**. There are different receptors for hot and cold. In human skin, as with most other mammals, these receptors have two limitations. Firstly, they tend to register temperature only relative to what the sensor has become used to, and so can give misleading signals. Secondly, outside a fairly narrow range of temperatures the pain receptors tend to do the sensing instead.

Pressure sensors allow the skin to register the degree of contact with another body, enabling us to grip and lift a bottle or lean against a wall.

Finally, other receptors register **pain**. They come into play when other 'touch' sensors have become overloaded (too much pressure, heat or cold). As with all of these receptors, there is a greater density of them in some skin areas than in others. There are further touch and pain receptors throughout the interior of the body.

Mammals have a range of highly developed sense organs which they use to gain information about their surroundings. Although all mammals have the same range of sense organs, particular organs are specially developed in certain mammals – for example, hearing in bats, smell in dogs, touch in moles and motion sensing in cats. An appreciation of the importance of their senses and what they can learn from them is essential for the children to become effective observers and scientists.

Why you need to know these facts

Pupil – the black centre of the eye that allows light through to the lens.
Iris – the coloured outer ring of the pupil that regulates the amount of light entering the eye.
Cornea – the tough outer covering of the eye.
Optic lens – the part of the eye that focuses light onto the retina.
Retina – the light-sensitive inner coating of the eyeball.
Cones – the colour-sensitive cells in the retina, only responsive to bright light.
Rods – retinal cells that are sensitive to motion, but not to colour.
Pinna – the outer portion of the ear.
Cochlea – the sound-sensitive part of the inner ear.

Vocabulary

Semicircular canals – the part of the inner ear that maintains balance by registering changes in position.
Echolocation – the use of echoed sounds to 'see' objects in the dark.
Taste buds – the taste-sensitive cells on the tongue and at the back of the mouth.

Amazing facts

● Some children with particularly sensitive hearing (mostly asthma sufferers) can hear frequencies up to 20kHz – but dolphins can respond to frequencies well above 100kHz.
● There are approximately 130 million light-sensitive cells on the retina of each human eyeball.
● In favourable conditions, wolves can detect the scent of their prey up to 2.5km away.
● When it is very dark, cats use their whiskers to feel their way around.

Common misconceptions

Bats are blind.
They are not blind, but they do find out more about their environment by building up a 'picture' from sound than by seeing. Their echolocation system is sensitive enough to enable them to catch a flying insect in the dark.

If you are colour blind, you only see in black and white.
Colour blindness usually means that one set of the light-sensitive cells is not working properly. The most common form is red-green blindness, which makes those two colours indistinguishable. In extremely rare cases, a person who is colour blind will only be able to see in shades of grey.

Questions

How does a dog track by smell?
The smell receptors in dogs (and cats as well – but they are much harder to train!) are very acute. The area within a dog's nose devoted to the sensing of odours is fifty times as large (with fifty times as many smell-sensitive cells) as the corresponding area in a human nose. Even the shape of a dog's nose is more conducive to the flow of smells than human nostrils. A dog is a thousand to a million times more sensitive to smells than a human.

Why do surgeons dress in green or blue?
When you are operating on someone, there tends to be quite a lot of blood around, so much of what the surgeons

are looking at will be red. After a while, their eyes will become less sensitive to so much red, making it more difficult for them to see what they are doing. To turn the red-sensitive cones in the eyes back 'on', the surgeons will look away from the operation for a brief moment and stare at something non-red – such as a green medical gown. When they look back to the operation, they will be able to see red once more.

Colour sensitivity (exploring, testing)

Ask the children to use coloured pens or coloured paper to make a cross in one colour (say red) on a white background. Ask them to stare at the cross for 30 seconds, then blink and look away at a plain white background. They should see a faint 'afterimage' of the cross, indicating the part of their retina where the red receptors have been 'turned down'. This afterimage should be a blue-green colour called cyan, the 'opposite' of red. The children can explore what other afterimages they can make themselves see. What colours are opposites? (Red and cyan; blue and orange; green and magenta.)

Sound location (exploring, modelling)

This activity is best done in a hall or gym. Blindfold a child and place him or her within a circle of other children. When you point to a child in the circle, they should click their fingers or tongue. Can the blindfolded child point to the source of the noise? This demonstrates how we can use our two ears to identify the direction of a sound.

Now blindfold a child and place him or her in a circle of children as above. Another child, without a blindfold, should now slowly walk around inside the circle. The blindfolded child says 'Ping', to which the other child replies 'Pong'. The blindfolded child then sets off in pursuit, walking slowly and 'pinging' in an attempt to locate and catch the other child, who must always respond immediately. This demonstrates how bats catch insects in the dark by echolocation.

Taste and smell (testing, sorting)

NB Make sure that standards of hygiene are maintained, and be aware of any food allergies. Supply the children with a variety of different flavours of crisps, presented in bowls without any labelling. Can they distinguish between the different flavours? Can they do so as accurately while holding their noses?

Taste and sight (testing, sorting)

NB Make sure that standards of hygiene are maintained, and be aware of any food allergies. You will need powdered mashed potato, some clear food flavourings (such as vanilla and peppermint) and some flavourless food colourings. Randomly colour and flavour some samples of potato. Ask the children to find out whether different colours of the same flavour taste 'different'. They will probably find that they do (even though they are the same flavour) – which demonstrates that we use different senses together to gain information about our world.

Smell matching (testing, sorting)

Provide a selection of different 'smelly' substances (such as spices and soaps) in opaque but open containers. Ask children to smell each substance without looking inside the pots: can they recognize and match different smells?

Concept 8: Mammalian life cycles

Subject facts

The key feature that sets mammals apart from other animals is the combination of live birth and initial feeding of the young from maternal mammary glands. The first stage of the life cycle of a mammal can be said to take place within the womb or **uterus**. All of the food and oxygen needs of the unborn **foetus** are supplied directly by the mother through the **placenta**: the foetus absorbs nourishment directly from the mother's blood supply.

Due to this relatively lengthy pre-birth growing period, mammals are born fully formed – though some require a long period of parental care before they can be left to fend for themselves. Depending on the environment that they are normally born into, a mammal may be capable of running with its parent to avoid predators within thirty minutes of birth, or be helpless (perhaps even blind) and dependent on the mother for anything from a few days up to several months.

In this infant stage, a mammal will depend entirely on the mother for nourishment in the form of milk. The number of **mammary** (milk-producing) **glands** on the adult female is usually closely linked to the number of infants likely to be born at any one time – if there are any more infants than that number, some are likely to die due to lack of access to food. Over a period of time, the infant will be weaned off the milk (usually to make way for another birth group) and will begin to accept a more adult diet. The extended period that mammals spend in family groups of this kind allows the young to learn from the adults. They will learn survival skills such as predator avoidance, food gathering and possibly social behaviours. During adolescence, most mammals become more independent; in some species, they will move (or be driven) away from their family groups entirely.

When a mammal reaches maturity, which could be weeks or years after birth depending on the species (the larger mammals usually take longer to mature), they will often establish their own family groups. This helps to prevent inbreeding, which (for genetic reasons) would be bad for the health of the group.

While in the mature, reproductive phase of their life cycle, most mammals change relatively little. The weakness brought about by old age will often result in the end of 'reproduction rights' and a change in lifestyle – but this depends on the social nature of the particular species. Some mammals support the elderly members of their family group for as long as possible, whereas others drive them away. There is still debate as to which of these categories humans fall into!

Why you need to know these facts

Most placental mammals progress through very similar developments within their life cycles. The level of parental care varies from species to species, but the initial maternal link is consistent. Most children will be aware of the stages of human development from their own experience, and can be encouraged to look for similarities and differences with other mammals. The life cycle of a non-placental mammal is discussed in Chapter 2.

Vocabulary

Infant – the stage of development immediately following birth, when there is still a high dependence on the mother or family group for nourishment.

Adolescent – an immature adult stage in which reproductive capability and other adult characteristics are developing.

Adult – the stage of development in which the individual is fully capable of reproduction.

(Also see vocabulary in Chapter 4.)

Mammals

- Some species of rat breed up to 13 times a year, with a maximum of 22 young in each litter. That's up to 286 young per mother in one year!
- A baby blue whale grows at a rate of 90kg per day.
- Elephants develop in the womb for almost 22 months, humans for nine months, and hamsters for 20 days.

Common misconceptions

For some common misconceptions and questions relating to the human life cycle, see Chapter 4 (pages 85).

Teaching ideas

Mammalian pets (observing, recording)
Those children with mammalian pets can be encouraged to keep records of their development (including photographs or videos) and to share these with the rest of the class.

Wildlife watch (observing)
An excellent range of wildlife videos are available that focus on a single family group of a particular species of mammal. This will give the children the opportunity, within a single lesson, to observe the yearly cycle of such a group. The children could go on to collect information about other mammal species, using books, CD-ROMs or the Internet.

Resources

The following will be useful for direct observation or research in the classroom:
- a body parts tabard with Velcro 'organs' that the children can place in position
- small mammal skeletons (cased)
- a plastic human skeleton (with internal organs)
- wildlife videos such as *Life on Earth*, *Super Nature* or the *National Geographic* series
- reference materials on the human body (also see Chapter 4) such as videos of the BBC series *The Human Body* and the Microsoft program *The Magic School Bus (Human Body)*
- CD-ROM nature encyclopaedias
- books on caring for pets.

Chapter 4
HUMANS

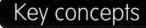

The study of humans forms the major part of the 'animal biology' content of the National Curriculum. Children should be expected to relate more readily to the 'human' elements of science, and then to link this knowledge to other aspects of zoology. To break the information into more manageable 'lumps', this chapter will only cover those aspects that are distinctive to humans. Those aspects of 'humans as organisms' (as detailed in the National Curriculum) which relate equally well to mammals in general are covered in Chapter 3. The key ideas to be developed here are:

1. Humans require a balanced nutritional diet of foods from several different food groups in order to grow and be healthy.
2. Exercise is important for the development of muscles and co-ordination skills.
3. Human reproduction and development can be described in terms of certain key stages.
4. Medicine is used to assist and supplement the mechanisms and processes of internal defence systems in fighting disease.
5. Humans are social animals, and their mental well-being and emotional needs are important aspects of their social existence.
6. Certain drugs can have harmful effects on humans.

Human life concept chain

For general comments on concept chains, see page 10.

KS1

Humans need food and water to stay alive. Humans need the right balance and amount of food to stay healthy. The right forms of exercise are important for healthy growth. Humans can produce babies. Human babies grow into children and then into adults. Some drugs are medicines and can be of benefit to particular individuals. Human children require adult care.

KS2

Food is necessary for human growth and activity. An appropriate balance of different food types is necessary for humans to remain healthy. It is possible to group foods in a number of different ways. Oral hygiene and dental care are important for digestion, and for medical and social reasons. Exercise and healthy eating are important to maintain human fitness, strength and stamina. Exercise has an effect on heart rate and breathing. Particular changes occur as humans progress from being babies to being children, adults and the elderly. The physical and emotional changes involved in growing up and ageing occur at different rates in different people. The human body has its own system of defences against diseases, and this system is assisted by a healthy and balanced lifestyle. Medicines can be dangerous when taken without supervision. Humans sometimes also use drugs, such as alcohol and tobacco, which have harmful effects.

KS3

The chemical components of different foods provide for different needs within the human body. The intake of food needs to be balanced against the energy requirements for physical activity. Appropriate levels of physical and mental activity are necessary for continued growth and development. The body's disease defence system operates at several different levels, depending upon the cause and site of an infection or illness. Medicines work in various ways. Humans progress through many different physical, emotional and mental changes as they age. Humans develop significantly between conception and birth. The male and female reproductive systems are significantly different in structure and operation. 'Recreational' drugs have specific short-term and long-term effects on the human body.

Food groups

There are various ways in which food can be categorized in terms of its nutritional value to us. However they are categorized, any one food (such as potato crisps) will fall into more than one category. A single piece of food may fit in to up to seven different nutritional categories:

● **carbohydrates** (eg starches and sugars) – used by the body to make energy
● **protein** (eg meat and cheese) – used by the body to manufacture and repair cells
● **fats** – used to make energy and store it in the body
● **minerals** (eg iron and calcium) – used in the manufacture of certain body parts, such as blood and bones
● **vitamins** – essential (in tiny amounts) for the health of the body
● **water** – the fluid in which all foods, once broken down, can be dissolved in order to be absorbed by the body
● **fibre** – aids the movement of food along the digestive tract.

Of these essential nutrients, water is the most important. Without it, a human would not be able to survive more than a few days. Although each category is important for the growth and maintenance of a healthy body, it would be possible to survive for some time (though not very healthily) if certain elements were missing from the diet. A protein-deficient diet, for example, will impair the body's ability to grow and repair damage. It is possible, depending on our level of activity, to survive for weeks or even months without food by consuming the food reserves that we carry around as fat and muscle.

There are two elements to a 'balanced diet':
● balancing energy input with energy usage (the more active you are, the more food you need)
● an appropriate balance between the food groups to ensure healthy growth and development.

Carbohydrates

These are basically the materials that plants are made from as a result of the process of **photosynthesis**, which combines carbon (from carbon dioxide in the atmosphere) with water (see Chapter 5, page 122). Carbohydrates are sometimes called 'sugars' – but according to this word use, there are 'fast sugars' and 'slow sugars' (or **simple** and **complex carbohydrates**). The words 'fast' and 'slow' refer to the rate of release within our digestive system. 'Fast sugars' are easily digestible and can start to be used by the body as energy within minutes of eating. 'Slow sugars' (or starches) require more digestion, so their energy release takes much longer. It's like the difference between an explosion and a sustained fire: the total energy released may be the same, but the rate of release is very different.

The reason that 'fast sugars' release their energy so readily is that they are relatively simple in structure. Examples are glucose, sucrose (cane sugar), fructose (fruit sugar), lactose and maltose. Glucose, being a **monosaccharide** (single sugar molecule), is the easiest of the sugars to digest; the others, including fructose, are **disaccharides** (double sugar molecules). When about 25 monosaccharides are linked together, a long-chain **polysaccharide** (starch) molecule is made. This is the chief means by which plants store energy. Animals use **glycogen**, a polysaccharide of about 10 molecules, to store their energy.

Plants also use a polysaccharide called **cellulose** for structural purposes: it provides the fibrous strengthening for plants. It is a very complex molecule, usually containing 200–300 monosaccharides. This complexity makes it all but impossible for humans to break down and use, though many animals can do so by means of a heavy-duty digestive system, often with a multi-chambered stomach. We can then eat these animals after they have turned the cellulose into meat.

Protein

The human body is about 50% protein (by dry weight). There are about 30 000 different proteins in our bodies, performing various different tasks – from muscle fibres to digestive enzymes and antibodies. Proteins are built up from **amino acids**, which are strands of carbon, oxygen, hydrogen and nitrogen atoms. The range of tasks that they perform within the body makes them essential for growth, repair, general maintenance and the healthy functioning of the body.

Plants produce all the amino acids that they need as a result of photosynthesis and the absorption of nitrogen through their roots (see Chapter 5, page 122). Humans (and other animals) can synthesize many of the 20 or so main amino acids; but there are eight, known as the 'essential amino acids', that humans cannot make. These have to be obtained from food. All of them can be found in plant seeds; but for two in particular (lysine and tryptophan), plants are not a very good source and can be supplemented by animal protein in the form of meat, eggs or dairy produce. It is recommended that babies receive 2.5g of protein for each kilogram of body weight per day. This is reduced to 1.5g and 0.8g per kilogram per day in children and adults respectively.

There are basically two types of protein: fibrous and globular. **Fibrous** proteins are made of twisted long-chain molecules and have a great strength: they form much of our muscle and skin tissue. **Globular** proteins can be carried in the blood; they include digestive enzymes, hormones (such as insulin), pigments (such as haemoglobin) and antibodies.

Fat

Weight for weight, **fat** is the most energy-rich food that we can eat. It contains over twice as much energy per gram as either protein or carbohydrate. There are three forms of fat in our diet: **monounsaturated** (olive and peanut oil), **polyunsaturated** (sunflower and corn oil, from which margarine is made) and **saturated** fats (red meat, dairy produce). Where there is a high energy need, due to either a high level of physical activity or a cold environment in which energy is required to maintain metabolism (body heat), an increased intake of dietary fat may not cause any harm.

The key health link is between fat and cholesterol. **Cholesterol** is a fatty substance required by the body to protect nerve fibres, build cell walls and produce certain hormones – but the liver is quite capable of producing all the cholesterol that the body requires, so we don't need to eat any extra. As fat doesn't dissolve in water, it requires special protein-based carriers (**lipoproteins**) to transport it around the body. Low-density lipoproteins (LDVs) take cholesterol out to the cell walls, and high-density lipoproteins (HDVs) scrape off the excess and return it to the liver for excretion via the digestive system.

Monounsaturated fats increase the proportion of LDVs, and the other fats increase the proportion of HDVs. If much more cholesterol is being taken out to the body than is required or can be brought back, then there is a build-up of cholesterol on the cell walls – particularly on the walls of veins and arteries. This build-up restricts the flow of blood through the vessels and increases the blood pressure (in order to get the same amount of blood through a smaller tube), putting a strain on the vessel walls and the heart – heart attack time! Intake of monounsaturated fats to produce more LDVs can, to a limited extent, counteract an excess of HDV-producing saturated fats.

In colder environments such as northern Canada and Scandinavia, where a high fat intake will quickly be converted into energy for maintaining metabolism, cholesterol is unlikely to be much of a problem. In Mediterranean Europe, fat intake has traditionally been confined to olive oil and moderate amounts of animal fat. With the warmer climate, far less energy is required to maintain metabolism (keep the body warm). In general, it is recommended that saturated fats should be avoided and polyunsaturated fats should not exceed 10% of the average energy intake. It is thought to be unsafe for fats (even monounsaturates) to exceed 30% of average energy intake.

Minerals

The body requires relatively small amounts of various metals to ensure the effective development and operation of particular parts of the body. But it won't do you much good to suck on a nail if you are anaemic (iron-deficient), as these **minerals** can only be absorbed as **salts**. Calcium, a mineral found in milk, is a key component in the proper formation and repair of bones and teeth. Common salt (sodium chloride) is necessary for the transmission of nerve impulses. No one food has all of the mineral salts that we require – hence the need for a varied and balanced diet (see below).

Vitamins

The human body, like that of any animal, relies on many interconnected chains of chemical reactions in order to function. **Vitamins** are chemicals that act as triggers for these reactions. The body only needs them in minute quantities; but if it is lacking in any one vitamin, whole chains of reactions can break down – which may lead to dangerous health problems. The table on page 92 shows a range of the vitamins that we require for good health, together with their common sources and the potential effects of deficiency. Vitamins enable the body to convert other foods into more useful forms. They assist in cell formation, nerve transmission and the formation of DNA.

The two vitamin groups, fat-soluble and water-soluble, differ in terms of intake and storage. **Fat-soluble** vitamins can be stored within fatty tissues in the body. This means that their intake can be infrequent, as long as it is enough to ensure that the necessary quantities are available. **Water-soluble** vitamins, on the other hand, cannot be stored: any excess is excreted in the urine. Intake of these vitamins thus has to be on a daily basis.

Some vitamins – particularly A, C, and E – help to counter the effects of potentially harmful chemicals known as **free radicals**. These chemicals, produced as an effect of toxic substances such as tobacco smoke, damage cells and make them more susceptible to cancer-causing agents.

Fibre

Dietary **fibre** is necessary for the efficient working of the digestive processes. Although it cannot be digested by humans (see page 62), it ensures that food keeps moving. At this point, the explanation becomes rather tasteless (no pun intended) – but necessary for an understanding of why so many breakfast cereal manufacturers spend so much time advertising foodstuffs that humans can't actually digest.

As the chyme (the slurry-like mix of food and digestive juices) works its way through the ileum to the colon, it relies on **peristalsis** (successive contractions of muscular rings around the digestive tract) to keep it moving. If this slurry is very fluid or is full of slippery fat, the peristalsis will not be effective, and so the food will take longer to make the digestive journey. That may not be too bad in the ileum, though it will cause a bit of 'backing up' (indigestion), but later on distinct problems will occur. In the colon, the water in the chyme is reabsorbed into the body to avoid dehydration (this is why you must drink but not eat when you are suffering from diarrhoea). If the movement through the colon is slowed because the inner walls cannot 'grip' the chyme to move it forward, then too much moisture will be extracted, making the stools harden and leading to a difficult or painful bowel movement (constipation). The addition of fibre to the diet causes the chyme to have more of a bulk, to knit together more, so that the action of peristalsis is more effective, movement is more assured, liquid re-absorption is at a more appropriate level, and... well, there you go!

I'm not sure what it is, but children seem to find descriptions like that fascinating! Granted, an excess of dietary fibre can cause a few practical (and social) problems: speeding up the digestive process will make bowel movements more frequent, with an increased likelihood of gaseous bowel discharge – but this is still quite a small price to pay for a vastly reduced likelihood of colonic cancers.

Classifying foods

It is not really possible to place individual foods into one group or another, because most foods contain so many

	VITAMIN	FOOD SOURCES	NEEDED FOR	EFFECTS OF DEFICIENCY
Fat-soluble	A	Green vegetables, dairy products, liver.	Components of retina in eye, skin condition.	Poor night vision, blindness, dry skin.
	D	Dairy products, eggs, cod liver oil. Produced by the skin in response to ultra violet light.	Growth and repair of bones.	Rickets (deformed bone growth).
	E	Seeds, leafy green vegetables.	Cell membranes.	Iron deficiency.
	K	Leafy green vegetables.	Blood clotting agents.	Excessive bleeding.
Water-soluble	B_1 (Thiamine)	Pork, grains, peas and beans.	Carbohydrate, metabolism, nerve and heart function.	Weakened heart, swelling, nerve and muscle degeneration.
	B_2 (Riboflavin)	Dairy products, liver, eggs, grains, pulses.	Energy metabolism.	Eye inflammation, poor skin condition.
	B_3 (Niacin)	Liver, lean meats, grains, pulses.	Cell respiration.	Skin and intestinal disorders.
	B_5 (Pantothenic acid)	Dairy products, liver, eggs, grains, pulses.	Energy metabolism.	Fatigue, loss of co-ordination.
	B_6 (Pyridoxine)	Grains, vegetables, meats.	Amino acid metabolism.	Convulsions, nervous irritability, kidney stones.
	C (Ascorbic acid)	Citrus fruits, leafy green vegetables, tomatoes.	Connective tissue in skin, blood vessels and teeth. May help in resisting infection.	Scurvy (breakdown of skin, blood vessels and teeth).
	Folic acid	Whole-wheat foods, green vegetables, pulses.	Nucleic acid metabolism.	Anaemia, diarrhoea.

elements. However, it is possible to say that particular foods provide more of one element than another. A useful way of sorting foods is the 'three Gs':

● 'Go' foods are the ones that provide energy for movement and activity – carbohydrates and fats (and proteins).
● 'Grow' foods are the ones that you need for bodily growth and development – proteins (and vitamins and minerals).
● 'Glow' foods are the ones that you need for health and maintenance – minerals, vitamins and fibre.

What should we eat?

Identifying 'good' and 'bad' foods is not the issue here: it is the **balance** of food types that is important.

Carbohydrates, in 'complex' forms such as such as bread, cereal, rice, potatoes and pasta, should provide all the energy requirements necessary in a slow release over the day. Sometimes there may be a need for a sugar 'boost' (headaches, shaking or feeling sick can indicate a drop in blood sugar level) between normal meal times, either just before or just after strenuous exercise. Eating food that requires a lot of digestion is not advisable just before exercise (it can lead to muscle cramps), so simple sugar foods are appropriate at this point; their energy value will be used almost immediately (but see Concept 2 below).

Protein sources, such as beans, nuts, fish, meat and dairy produce, will provide most of the 'building materials' that the body requires (as well as providing vitamins and minerals). Red meat and dairy produce, because of their saturated fat content, should be eaten in moderation unless you are particularly active and likely to 'burn off' the energy value of the fat content.

Sources of vitamins and minerals, in particular fresh fruit and vegetables (which also have a considerable carbohydrate content) should be a regular part of any diet. Non-fresh or processed fruit and vegetables may have a reduced nutritional value; and over-cooking also reduces the useful food content.

Fats are not necessary as a specific component of a healthy diet. The small amount of monounsaturated fat (or oil) that you do require can be obtained from food such as nuts, dairy produce and some fruits and vegetables (such as olives). The fat in most processed foods is usually of the less useful polyunsaturated or saturated variety.

Fibre is contained in most basic foods, as long as they are not over-processed or over-cooked. Cereals and green vegetables are an excellent source of dietary fibre; but cereals may have been processed to have most of the fibre content removed (the bran is then often sold back to you in a separate packet!), and over-boiling vegetables breaks down the structure of the cellulose (that's why boiled cabbage goes limp and floppy). Beware of processed snacks such as crisps: they may be based on the fibrous potato, but they have a fat content of up to 45%!

Malnutrition

Malnutrition is often perceived to be a problem caused by lack of food, but it is correctly defined as 'a deficiency or excess of one or more essential nutritional elements within a diet'. Since the lack (or excess) of different nutritional elements will lead to different symptoms, it is impossible to say what somebody suffering from malnutrition will look like. Using the definition given above, most of the population of the world can be described as malnourished: they eat too much of some things and/or too little of others.

The food most commonly eaten in excess is fat. The average citizen of the USA will receive almost 40% of his or her daily energy intake in the form of simple processed sugars, 40% as fats and less than 20% as complex carbohydrates. Ideally, over 50% of energy intake should come from complex carbohydrates and less than 10% from fats. In industrialized countries, there is also an increasing reliance on food supplements (vitamin and mineral tablets) to counteract a lack of fresh fruit and vegetables. Recent research has noted that the diet of British children was more balanced at the end of the 1940s than at the end of the 1990s.

Starvation is an extreme form of malnutrition in which the body has suffered a deficiency of essential nutritional elements for a sustained period of time. When starvation begins, body fat is converted to provide energy; once this supply is exhausted, muscle tissue and internal organs begin to be converted and therefore shrink. More fluid is retained as internal systems begin to degenerate – this causes the distended stomach often associated with victims of starvation. The body loses its ability to repair itself and fight infection: illnesses such as respiratory infections and gastroenteritis, brought on by starvation, are the world's biggest killers of infants and young children.

Towards a balanced diet

The key to a healthily balanced diet is to consume a variety of food types. Neither chocolate nor lettuce will provide all that a growing child needs, but both have their value in the overall make-up of a diet. Certain vitamins and minerals are essential, and most of these can be obtained by eating a range of fruit and vegetables. Protein can be obtained from a range of sources, but will not be eaten in isolation from other food types (fat in meat, carbohydrate in cereal). Clearly, an over-indulgence in simple sugars or fats will not be good; but over-eating within any food group will lead to problems.

In general, if your intake of energy (food) is greater than your use of energy (exercise), the excess will be stored as fat. It is only when intake falls below usage that the fat will begin to be converted back into energy. Beyond this, starvation sets in as muscle tissue is converted into energy in order to maintain metabolism. The balance of energy intake and usage is a fine one to manage, and taking appropriate exercise is at least as important.

Eating disorders

Obesity is a growing problem throughout the western world. It is caused as much by a sedentary lifestyle and poor dietary habits as by an increase in overall energy intake. The best solutions to this problem are education towards a reduced reliance on processed foods that contain high levels of simple sugars and fats, and increased acceptance, at a social level, of the need for exercise and physical activity.

The pressure of social norms and media-driven ideals of acceptable body shape has led to an increased frequency, mainly in young females, of cases of **anorexia nervosa** and **bulimia nervosa**. Although these are different conditions, both tend to result from the fear of becoming obese or the irrational need to reduce weight based on a poor self-image. There are a range of body shapes within the band of 'normality', the key aspect being that they are neither too fat nor too thin – both extremes are equally unhealthy.

Nutritional value

On all packaged foods, there will be a nutritional information panel which provides data concerning the energy, protein, carbohydrate, fat and fibre contents for a given amount of the food (usually either 100g or 100ml). In most cases the carbohydrates will be divided into sugar and starch. Sometimes the fat will be identified as either saturated or unsaturated. This allows comparisons to be made between the nutritional values of different foods. Where vitamins are included, the percentage of the recommended daily allowance (RDA) per portion or given amount of food will be stated too.

Children are constantly receiving an almost incomprehensible range of messages about what they eat, especially from advertisements. Science needs to offer them a means of deciding for themselves what they should be eating. An understanding of the key food groups and their effects on growth and body maintenance, and of how individual dietary requirements are balanced against activity levels, is an important factor in their general health awareness. With the growing number of food 'health scares', children need to have a balanced view in order to understand issues that arise – from GM soya to particular religious taboos.

Vocabulary

Nutrition – the way in which we (and other living things) gain energy from food.

Carbohydrates (such as starches and sugars) – foods used by the body to make energy.

Proteins (such as meat and cheese) – foods used by the body to manufacture and repair cells.

Fats – energy-rich foods which represent special energy stores in an animal or plant.

Minerals (such as iron and calcium) – trace elements in foods, used in the manufacture of certain body parts (for example, blood and bones).

Vitamins – chemicals in foods that are essential (in small quantities) for the physical well-being of the body.

Water – the fluid in which all of the above, after digestion, are dissolved in order to be absorbed by the body.

Fibre – indigestible material that aids the movement of food along the digestive tract.

Cholesterol – a fatty substance that preserves nerve fibres.

Peristalsis – muscular action to move food along the digestive tubes.

Malnutrition – the effects of a poorly balanced or inadequate diet.

Starvation – the effects of a prolonged lack of food.

Amazing facts

● The heaviest person on record weighed 635kg in 1978 – at one stage, 91kg was gained in one week (mainly due to fluid retention). The same person then lost 419kg over a two-year period under strict medical supervision.

● In 1979, a man in Austria survived without food or water after being locked in a police cell and forgotten about for 18 days.

Sweet things are not good for you.

Strictly speaking, it should be: *Eating a lot of sweet things is not good for you.* Sugary food is only appropriate if the energy derived from it is to be used immediately (otherwise it will be stored in the body as fat), so sweets must be balanced with activity! The sugar content of the sweets can damage teeth, but this effect can be countered by a good dental hygiene regime.

The more vitamins you eat, the fitter you will be.

The body has different daily requirements for different vitamins. Exceeding these required intakes is not necessarily better still; in fact, overdosing on certain vitamins may actually be harmful. In any case, fitness is not just about an appropriate intake of vitamins: without a balanced diet and sufficient exercise, physical fitness will not be achieved.

Why is breakfast 'the most important meal of the day'?

Coming after a period of inactivity (sleep) during which the final stages of digestion have usually reached their conclusion, the body usually has an 'empty' feeling about it. More importantly, breakfast normally precedes a period of physical activity. It is an opportunity to build up usable energy stores by eating food rich in carbohydrates (such as toast or cereal) for release during the day. Food eaten late at night, on the other hand, is more likely to be converted into fat, because during sleep there isn't a great need for the energy.

Questions such as 'Am I fat?' and 'Do I need to lose weight?' must be treated with care and sensitivity: the emphasis should be on improving self-image. It may more appropriate to increase the level of activity through exercise or to improve the balance of the diet (both of which will help to build confidence) than to 'go on a diet'. Often it is a case of eating 'better' rather than 'less'.

Favourite foods (recording, researching)

Ask the children to draw their favourite meal and then to find out its relative nutritional value using reference sources. Is it a reasonable balance of food groups? How could it be changed to provide a better balance?

Food diary (recording, presenting)

The children could keep a diary of their eating habits for one week and compare this with the recommended balance of foods. Are there any food groups that they are consistently missing out on? **NB** Be sensitive to the fact that many children have little control over the range of food that they eat.

Food collage (classifying, recording)

Draw a large Venn diagram with three intersecting circles labelled 'Go', 'Grow' and 'Glow'. Discuss with the children where various foods should be placed on the chart. Working together, place and then attach food packets in the most appropriate places. Are there any packets that are outside all three sets? (Some 'snacks' may fall into this category.) How many of these foods simply provide energy (sugar and fat)?

Nutritional charts (researching, classifying, data handling, presenting)

Working in groups, the children can look at the nutritional information panels from several similar food products such as breakfast cereals, biscuits or chilled desserts (a different type for each group), then collate and present the information using tables and graphs. They can use this data to compare the amounts of energy, protein and other dietary elements provided by each product. More able children could record the data on a computer spreadsheet and convert it to graphs.

Sorting cereals (classifying, data handling)

The children can input nutritional data from several different cereal packets on to a computer spreadsheet, then use this to answer questions such as: *Do 'brand name' and 'own brand' cereals of the same type (such as corn flakes) have the same nutritional content? Which is the highest fibre cereal? Which contains the most/least sugar?* What questions can the children come up with?

Rich foods (interrogating data, classifying)

Choose a food group (such as protein or fibre) and search through the nutritional information panels on food packages that the children have brought in to find 'high' and 'low' examples. Repeat with other food groups, asking questions such as: *Which food has the highest sugar content? Which food package admits to having the greatest proportion of saturated fats?*

'Trumps' (researching, comparing)

Play 'trumps' with cards made from nutrition information panels from different food packages. Choose a food category (such as protein); each player lays down a card, then the player whose card shows the highest protein content wins and calls the next 'trump' category. The food products could be similar in nature (such as breakfast cereals or chocolate biscuits), or be very different.

Concept 2: Exercise and physical activity

'Automatic' movements

Subject facts

Many of the movements that we take for granted are anything but automatic when we learn them. After spending a considerable portion of your life (well, it probably seems so at the time) desperately pulling yourself to a standing position, you soon get the hang of the 'balancing and walking around' idea. But actually observing what you do, examining each small movement in detail, helps you to realize what a difficult thing it must have been to begin with. The central nervous system stores up these habitual movements as **subroutines**: embedded, semi-automatic functions.

The concentration and co-ordination needed to direct a spoonful of food successfully into the mouth is initially great. By the age of eight or nine, children (or so I've noticed with my own two) are capable not only of feeding themselves, but also of balancing on one leg of their chair and watching TV at the same time! However, I have also noticed that there are times when – rather in the way that a computer 'locks up' if you run too many programs at the same time – my children 'lock up' with food halfway to their mouths whenever there's a particularly exciting piece of TV that requires their full attention. What amuses me most is when the fork finally reaches the mouth, the 'automatic' chewing action begins and a frown spreads across the face, denoting 'there's something wrong here', as they realize that the food has dropped off somewhere between plate and mouth.

The key point here is that actions become more precise and less conscious with practice. Sports coaches often say things like 'It's important not too think too hard about it' or

'Don't think about hitting the ball, just hit it'. This is because if we focus on every little movement we take as part of a bigger action, the brain will tend to get in the way. The subroutines or automatic systems need to be allowed to do their job. Generally, the more we practise, the more embedded an activity becomes, and the better (or faster) it can be performed.

Fitness

With repetition of particular movements there is not only an increase in the level of skill, but also an increase in the level of **fitness** – that is, the combination of strength, suppleness and endurance (see illustration). Muscles only develop when they are used: if you do not perform particular movements for a long period of time (for example, if you lie in bed for a number of weeks), the unused muscles will deteriorate. Where an activity is repeated, however, there will be muscle formation to support that movement. The type of muscle formed may allow the movement to be performed more quickly, more strongly or for longer (or a combination of the three). The muscles used will also recover more quickly from their exertion. In this way, we adjust to become 'fitter'. To ensure all-round fitness, we need a pattern of exercise that develops the full range of muscle groups.

Energy delivery

The key to overall fitness is the heart. This delivers oxygenated blood to the muscles, enabling them to convert energy into movement (see the sections on movement and respiration in Chapter 3, pages 53). To get the blood to the muscles when it is needed, the heart needs to pump faster and/or pump a greater volume of blood. Sustained exercise, involving exertion for twenty minutes at a time, can make the heart stronger so that it will beat faster and more powerfully. By increasing the amount of oxygenated blood being delivered to the muscles, the period for which the muscles can respire aerobically can be increased.

If the muscles are not able to convert energy fast enough aerobically, they will begin **anaerobic respiration**. This will result in a build-up of lactic acid in the muscles, causing the 'tired' feeling. When the activity ends, the need to remove the accumulated lactic acid will cause a continued need for oxygen (panting) and increased blood flow (elevated heart rate) until the muscles return to normal. The less fit you are, or the less efficient your heart is at delivering oxygenated blood, the sooner you will move into anaerobic

weightlifter   distance runner   gymnast

respiration and the longer it will take to recover from it.

The measurable effects of sustained exercise are that the heart can beat faster under strain, it can return to the 'at rest' rate sooner, and the 'at rest' rate itself is slower (the heart doesn't need to beat as often to pump the same amount of blood). As you progress into an exercise regime, it is possible to chart your improved **cardiovascular** (heart and circulatory) fitness by measuring these three indicators.

Flexibility

Suppleness – the ability to stretch and move to the extremes that our joints will allow without being injured – is also a benefit of exercise. The stretching of muscles in a 'warm-up' prior to vigorous exercise is particularly important if muscle damage is to be avoided. Progressively and gently stretching the muscles causes their fibres to 'warm up' (their metabolic rate is increased), allowing them to increase their uptake of oxygen from the bloodstream. This preparation helps to prevent the muscles from becoming overstrained when they are put under pressure during activity. This is as true for the heart as for any other muscle.

As well as increasing the bulk of muscles, repetitive exercise can also increase their length. Muscles and tendons attach one bone to another across a joint (see Chapter 3, page 47). If they are not regularly stretched, both will gradually shorten to restrict movement around the joint. Regular, gentle stretching exercises will increase suppleness, ensuring freedom of movement and mobility of the joints.

Exercise and diet

Exercise and diet work together to ensure that the energy consumed is equal to the energy used. The more exercise is carried out, the more energy-giving food is required – but as soon as the level of exercise is reduced, there must be a corresponding decrease in food intake if an increase in body weight is to be avoided. When we are trying to develop general fitness, strength and suppleness, we need to increase our intake of growth foods (proteins) in order to build more body tissue where required.

A further nutritional requirement of increased activity is an increase in the level of water intake. This directly increases blood plasma levels, improving the transportation of nutrients around the body and helping to filter out the waste by-products of physical activity (heat and urea). Sipping small amounts of water frequently is the best way of maintaining a balanced fluid level.

Why you need to know these facts

In the drive towards educating children to develop a fit, healthy body within a healthy lifestyle, exercise and diet are key elements. Along with an appropriate and balanced food intake, there needs to be an appropriate level of activity to make good use of the energy intake. An understanding of the physiological aspects of exercise should be taught in conjunction with a policy and curriculum for physical education that aims to develop fitness in terms of physical co-ordination, stamina and strength.

Vocabulary

See Chapter 3, page 42, for definitions of aerobic and anaerobic respiration.

Amazing facts

When you are at rest, it will take one minute for all of the blood in your body to pass through your heart. Intense exercise will greatly reduce the time. Some of the world's fittest athletes (mainly cyclists) can pump it through in 15 seconds when they need to!

You have to be slim or muscular to be fit.
Fitness has more to do with the internal workings of the
body than with the outward appearance. A muscular body
means that one aspect of fitness – strength – has been
developed; there may not be a corresponding level of
endurance or suppleness. Similarly, there is no clear link
between slimness and muscle tone. Someone who looks a
little overweight (but not obese) is just as likely to be fit as a
supermodel.

You can 'eat yourself fit'.
Diet certainly has a role in developing fitness, but fitness
doesn't happen without regular, aerobic exercise: activity
that raises the heart rate for sustained periods of 20 to 30
minutes each day (such as fast walking, jogging, cycling or
swimming).

Can exercise be bad for you?
In the same way that it is recommended that you eat more
of some foods than of others, some forms of exercise are
more appropriate than others. More strenuous or longer-
duration activities should be built up slowly, and should
focus on a full range of muscle areas. Attempting to do too
much too soon or approaching exercise in short, sharp
bursts is likely to result in exhaustion and strained muscles.

Does a fast heartbeat mean that you are not fit?
It depends **when** the heart is beating faster. The fitter you
are, the slower your heart will beat when you are resting –
but the faster it will beat when you are exercising
vigorously, and the faster it will return to the rest rate when
you stop the exercise. A fit heart muscle will not have to
beat as often to pump the same amount of blood around the
body, so a fitter person will have a slower heart rate at rest
than the same person would if they were less fit.

It is important not to overstress the children or require
them to perform activities that are currently beyond their
abilities. Differences in physical ability between the
children need to be treated with sensitivity.

How to walk (sequencing, recording)
Walking might seem easy – but could the children tell a
robot how to walk? Let them work in pairs, giving and

following instructions, then writing down an agreed set.
Can they give instructions for other movements?

Movement and muscles (observing)

Encourage the children to be aware of all the co-ordinated
movements that are necessary to pick up a pencil, or to
stand up and sit down. Performing these actions in slow
motion will increase their motor control and allow them to
focus on different aspects. Which particular muscles are
involved? How are these muscles controlled?

Stretchy legs (comparing, recording)

This activity can be linked to PE. Ask the children to sit on
the floor with their legs stretched out in a V, then to walk
their hands forward, bending at the waist until the backs of
their legs feel tight – they can stop there! Measure how far
they have reached forward. Repeat this every day for a few
weeks: are they able to reach further by the end? Are some
children more supple than others?

Heart rate (measuring, recording)

The children can find and record their pulse rates by
measuring the number of wrist pulses (see illustration) in
15 seconds, then multiplying by 4. Encourage them to
participate in some fairly vigorous
aerobic activity. They should record
their pulse rate for the first 15
seconds after stopping, then for 15
seconds in every minute for the
next five minutes. What is their
peak pulse rate? How soon do they
return to the 'at rest' rate? Within a
PE programme, this activity may be
repeated over a period of six weeks
or more to help the children chart
their fitness development.

Where on
the wrist the pulse is

Aerobic exercises (planning, researching)

Groups of children can research different forms of aerobic
exercise (using encyclopaedias or textbooks) and plan an
exercise routine, working on a range of different areas of
the body with full warm-up and cool-down sections.
Compare the groups' results. Are there any similarities
between their programmes? Are some elements or body
areas common to all the programmes (for example, an
increased heart rate)? Is there a difference between the
'fitness' elements and the 'strength' elements?

Children's awareness of reproduction, birth and growth

Not long after the birth of our first child, I noted that three of the eight reception children at my school had mothers who were pregnant. After some careful, roundabout questioning, all three acknowledged that their mothers had 'babies in their tummies'. When asked how the baby would get out, one child said that Mum was going into hospital to have it removed. Another told me about a 'special hole' between Mum's legs. The third child burst into tears, clearly having worried about the problem for some time: Mum's tummy kept getting bigger and there was no way that the baby would fit through her belly button, leaving only one option – Mum was going to explode! (A number of mothers whom I have since regaled with this anecdote have said: 'The third kid's not far wrong'.) A brief chat with the mother concerned helped me to realize how unaware many parents assume their children to be, and how difficult they can find it to talk to their children about 'certain things'.

By approaching reproduction and growth from this starting point, you are focusing on an event of immediate interest to a large number of children. In my experience, children aged three to five show surprisingly little interest in how a baby 'gets in there', so discussion can focus on birth and the first year or so of life. The explanation that 'there's a special hole between Mum's legs' is usually sufficient to explain how the baby will be born – but the addition of 'When it's ready, it will start pushing so Mum will know' is usually wise, or you might have children worrying even more! You can also rely on the knowledge of other children to further the discussion – 'Mum said I was born in the middle of Tesco's'; 'My Mum had an operation when my little sister was born'; and so on. These anecdotes can be used to further the discussion, with the children explaining and you correcting where necessary.

A new baby's needs are often difficult for an older child to come to terms with, especially when they haven't shared their parent(s) before. If you can persuade a mother (or father) to bring their new arrival into school for a group of children to look at, and to answer questions about what the baby does and needs, the experience can be enlightening for all concerned. My personal favourite was a question put to the mother of a three-month-old baby: 'Does he eat crisps?' 'No, I'm still feeding him.' 'What flavour crisps are you feeding him then?' Young children are often quite surprised by the helplessness of babies and the constant care and attention that they require. (This is a very telling point to make with twelve- to fourteen-year-olds as well!) Sleeping and feeding patterns are quite important to the children, as the situation may be seen as 'unfair' – 'He's only a baby, but I have to go to bed before him'; 'She eats all the time, but I have to wait for tea'. By talking these points through, the children can come to a better understanding of a baby's needs and a greater sense of shared responsibility.

By the end of Key Stage 1, children can begin to look back over their lives and identify key developmental points: walking, speaking, starting school, reading, riding a bike. They can begin to associate 'growing up' with themselves by noting things that they are now able to do but couldn't do before. There may be an awareness of changes in their own bodies: more balance, greater control, different proportions. They are also likely to become more aware of differences between their own and other children's bodies: gender, overall size and shape, colour, physical abilities. The idea that everyone is built to the same basic design, but that each person is unique, can be developed from here.

By Key Stage 2, children are becoming more aware of themselves as individuals. This self-consciousness may lead them to exaggerate the differences between themselves and others, with either positive or negative results. Rates of growth begin to be an issue: some children may be growing faster than others, and some parts may be growing faster than others. There may be considerable concern about what is 'normal' – and between eight and eighteen, this has to be tackled **very** broadly from physical, social and emotional perspectives. It is impossible to deal with all of these issues from a scientific or teaching point of view here; and many are also subject to particular religious factors. As a former teacher of this age group, I would stress the importance of teaching the physical in the context of emotional and social considerations, and emphasizing the importance of a stable family situation (whatever form the family unit might take).

During Key Stage 2, as well as looking back, children should be looking into their dim and distant future: adulthood. The changes undergone between childhood and adulthood are significant – not only physical changes, but emotional ones with new levels of responsibility. Children should begin to compare themselves not only with young adults (18–35), but also with middle-aged adults (35–55) and those in old age. (See illustration.) Expectations about physical and emotional changes should be identified and

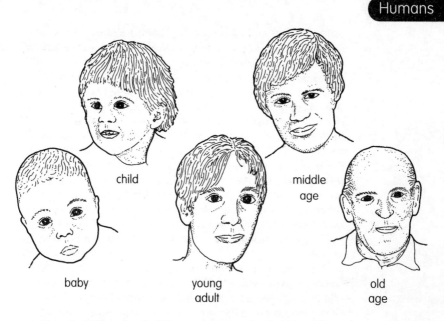

child

middle age

baby

young adult

old age

considered. Although all of these points are relative, and subject to considerable bias and stereotyping, the differences considered might include physical strength and stamina; suppleness and flexibility; mental agility and concentration; and long- and short-term memory.

Human reproduction

Males, from a purely physical point of view, are usually capable of taking part in reproductive activity from the point that they reach maturity until they die. Male reproductive maturity is not usually achieved before the age of ten or eleven, and will depend on nutrition and hereditary factors. **Sperm**, the male contribution to reproduction, are continually produced in the **testes**, which are suspended in a sac called the **scrotum** to keep them a couple of degrees Celsius below normal body temperature. The sperm are mixed with a watery fluid to produce **semen**, which is retained within the body until it is ejaculated through the **penis**. This may happen unconsciously during sleep or as a direct result of stimulation. There are something like 300 million sperm in each ejaculation.

Once the sperm have been delivered to the passage leading to the organ that contains the female eggs, the male role in reproduction (from a purely genetic perspective) has been completed. Although males are capable of producing sperm throughout their lives, there is recent evidence that the sperm count declines in later years (anything less than 5 million per ejaculation is classed as sub-fertile) and that sperm produced by older men have a greater proportion of genetic defects.

Females are born with a fixed number of eggs. These are released in a regular cycle of approximately one per month, starting soon after reaching maturity and ending when hormonal changes cause it to cease (some time between the mid-forties and the mid-fifties). In a 28-day cycle, the first five days will consist of the breakdown and release of the lining of the **uterus**, which will flow out of the **vaginal passage**. During days 6 to 13, the lining of the uterus is renewed and thickened with a rich blood covering. Hormonal signals then trigger **ovulation**: the release of a mature egg or **ovum** from the ovarian sacs. During days 15 to 28, the egg floats down the **fallopian tube** and enters the uterus.

If a sperm impregnates the egg during this period, the fertilized ovum will attach itself to the wall of the uterus, where it will begin to grow into an **embryo**. Hormonal changes will cause the growth of the **placenta**, through which the embryo will derive nourishment. If a sperm does not impregnate the egg, or the ovum does not attach to the lining of the uterus, the lack of hormonal signals will prevent the lining of the uterus from developing further, and it will be discarded at the start of the next cycle.

The rate of growth, starting with a single impregnated egg cell, is very impressive. By about five weeks, the embryo is just big enough to be seen; it has specialized cell growth, so that the body, head and internal organs have all begun to develop. After eight weeks, it is recognizable as something vaguely animal-like, with arms, legs and eyes – it is now called a **foetus**. At 12 weeks, it is moving around and has become recognizably male or female. By 16 weeks, it is about 15cm long and has begun to stretch the uterus. Eight weeks later, it will have doubled in size and will have periods of activity and rest; it now responds to sounds from outside the mother's body. During the last month in the uterus, the baby will practise doing useful things such as sucking its thumb and will put on some body fat.

The mother, through the **umbilical cord**, provides all the nourishment and oxygen that the baby needs, and takes away all of the waste products. This dependency continues until birth (though some mothers claim that it continues until at least the mid-twenties). The uterus, which at the start of pregnancy was about the size of a small pear, ends up just prior to birth as big as a basketball. During birth, the muscular walls of the uterus contract to ease the baby out.

Once a human reaches full sexual maturity there is a phase – generally between 18 and 35, although this will depend on many factors, including genetics, nutrition and general health and fitness – in which the body reaches a peak of performance. Beyond this, there is a steady decline as parts of the body begin to wear out and repair is less effective. There are only so many times that cells within the body can successfully divide in order to replace lost cells. Genetic errors begin to creep in, and the body begins to age. Beyond the age of 55 or so, irreversible changes will have begun to take place: female reproduction may no longer be possible, joints may have begun to degenerate, and skin will be less flexible. If the cells could be made to continue dividing for longer, the incidence of cellular degradation would be reduced and the effects of ageing delayed.

Why you need to know these facts

Children can become very concerned about birth and the early stages of development, especially when it is happening in their family. It is quite likely that children will gain siblings while they are aged between three and five – and if they are not adequately prepared, this can become quite a traumatic event in their young lives. Appropriate education can help them to understand the changes in mother and baby, and the changes at other points in their own physical development and maturation.

From the teacher's perspective, it is a matter of choosing the right time and vocabulary to talk these things through with the children. Any discussions of this kind should be carried out in accordance with your school's policy on sex education. Parents should at least be pre-warned; at best, they should be involved in detailed discussion of the intended programme. Because of these complexities, this section focuses on the likely misconceptions and pedagogical issues as well as the biological facts.

Sexual reproduction – the combining of genetic material from two individuals to produce a new life.
Sperm – a mobile cell which contains the male contribution to reproduction.
Ovum – the egg; the female contribution to reproduction.
Uterus – a special organ in the female abdomen which provides an environment for the developing embryo and foetus.
Embryo – the early stage of development of the fertilized ovum.

Foetus – the later, distinctively human phase of development of the embryo leading up to birth.
Placenta – a growth within the uterus that provides the foetus with its blood supply.

Amazing facts

● Human females seldom have more than 400–450 fertile periods (each lasting 24–48 hours) in their lifetime, whereas the average contents of one male ejaculation provides sufficient sperm to replace the population of most of Western Europe.
● Nearly 80% of the world's centenarians (people aged over 100) are female.

Common misconceptions

Misconceptions from parents
Sex education is all about conception and contraception.
During the later pre-teens and teens, this will probably be the case; but parents of younger children must be reassured that this content is not the entirety of the subject. Teachers need to take parents carefully through the potential lines of development that the topic will take during Key Stages 1 and 2. If teaching reveals that a child has knowledge concerning sexual practices well beyond the expectations for that age, the teacher and headteacher will need to consider carefully where the child obtained that knowledge.

Misconceptions from children
Babies can't talk because they have small brains.
Humans are born with some abilities and have to learn others. Babies are born with the ability to make a noise, but it takes time for them to learn how to communicate with words. It has nothing to do with brain size: it has to do with the amount of time that it takes to learn a complex new skill.

Questions

Questions asked by adults
Do I have to teach sex education?
The absolute answer is probably no – but this question may indicate a misconception about what is supposed to be taught. A surprisingly large amount of the early 'sex education' content can be taught through the general class ethos – relationships, caring for others – and through

discussion, rather than through explicit factual teaching. Please refer to school policies and government guidance.

Can I withdraw my child from sex education lessons?
Technically, yes – but are the parents clear about what they are actually withdrawing their child from? It is likely that this question indicates a misconception about what the content will be. Also, given that the teaching in question is likely to be embedded in general class sessions rather than in neatly packaged 'sex education lessons', withdrawal of a child may present practical problems.

Questions asked by children
My mum has just had twins – how did two babies get in there?
Sometimes two (or more) eggs are released at the same time and, if fertilized, they both grow into babies. These will be non-identical twins, because they have come from different eggs. Sometimes a single egg, very soon after it begins to grow into a baby, splits into two and both parts grow into babies. When this happens, the twins will be identical: they will look almost exactly the same.

Interviews (questioning, researching)
Ask the children to devise questions to ask a mother with a young baby about the baby's physical and mental abilities. Can they devise similar questions to ask a middle-aged person and an elderly person about themselves? Clearly, some editorial control will be required; but the key is for the children to identify the changes, and to note similarities and differences with their own circumstances. Invite appropriate people in, and conduct class or group interviews.

Age collage (classifying, observing)
The children can cut out and mount photographs of people of different ages, either in sequential order or in sets to represent different age groups. In the latter case, discuss with the class what these age groups should be.

Can do/can't do (observing, matching)
Make a class list of things that humans of various ages are able to do: go to the toilet themselves, feed themselves, walk, have children and so on. Link these statements to magazine photos of different-aged people. The effects of old

age will need to be discussed with the class, as abilities can vary greatly: an elderly relative who is fit and active will need to be considered at the same time as a more senile elderly relative.

Timeline (sequencing, recording)

The children can produce their own personal timelines, incorporating photographs and key dates (which do not need to be exact) relating to their own physical development – for example, when they first walked, talked or rode a bike. This activity could be extended by using scanned images to produce a computer presentation; the file could be developed into a web page with hyperlinked pages containing greater detail.

Concept 4: Medicines

Subject facts

Non-prescription medicines

The availability and use of non-prescription (or 'over the counter') medicines needs to be discussed. Children should only ever take these under the direction of a responsible adult. They need to be aware of the occasions when it is appropriate to take such medicines, and the potential consequences of misuse. Most drugs of this type are either **painkillers** (aspirin, paracetamol) or **antiseptics** (Savlon, TCP), and are either intended for general use or have age-specific ('adult' and 'junior') versions.

Another important distinction is between medicines for oral use and those for external use (for example, painkillers and antiseptics respectively) External medicines are safe if they are only applied externally and key instructions (such as 'not to be used on broken skin') are followed. Oral medicines are designed to be taken in particular dosages: the maximum dosage and lower age limit are displayed on the container. For this reason, medicines should always be kept in their original containers. Where available, the 'child' version of a medicine should be used (for example, Calpol for paracetamol).

Most oral drugs have a stated maximum intake, both per dose and over a given period. These safety limits have to be very strict, and most types normally taken by children are not likely to cause more than drowsiness or an upset stomach if taken in excess. An important exception is paracetamol: a significant excess of this can cause irreparable damage to the liver.

Most painkillers work by interfering with pain reception or transmission, or by reducing inflammation around the painful area. Antiseptics work by killing the microbes that might cause infection.

Prescription medicines

The use of **antibiotics** to kill microbes that cause various inflammations (such as sore throats, earache and septic toes) makes them quite familiar. This familiarity can result in inappropriate use. Antibiotics should always be used for their full course, and any remaining unused doses should be disposed of. Only the person that they are prescribed for should ever use them: many people are allergic to some antibiotics, so exposure to the wrong antibiotic can do far more harm than good.

With the increased identification and treatment of childhood asthma, **inhalant** drugs are becoming more widely recognized in schools. The drugs used will either reduce the possibility of a spasm or inhibit inflammation of the bronchial tubes. If taken by another asthmatic, the medication may be delivered in the wrong dosage.

Immunization

Treating children with a **vaccine** can now prevent many transmittable childhood illnesses such as rubella, chickenpox, polio and measles. A vaccine contains a weaker version of the disease-causing particles or **antigens**. The body can fight these off quite easily – and it then 'remembers' how to make the defence agents or **antibodies** required to fight off the illness without actually catching it. If the vaccinated child is exposed to the illness, the necessary antibodies will be reproduced in such number that the infection will not be developed. The child can then be said to be **immune** to that illness. Some diseases (such as chickenpox) leave the sufferer immune to the disease in the future.

If an unvaccinated child is infected with the illness, it will take some time for the body to develop the necessary antibodies, and so the illness will run its full course. In extreme cases, where the antibodies have not been produced, the illness can become more serious; for example, if the measles virus spreads to the brain, it may cause brain damage or even death. Although cases of adverse reaction to a **vaccination** have been noted, the risk of serious, lasting problems as a result of such a reaction is much less and much rarer than the risk from the illness itself.

Hormone deficiencies

The particular deficiency that children are most likely to come across is lack of **insulin** in the illness **diabetes**. Insulin controls the amount of glucose being absorbed by the body tissues for conversion to energy. If glucose cannot be absorbed, it continues to build up in the blood and must be excreted in urine, leading to excess urination and hence to dehydration and thirst. A direct injection of insulin will allow the glucose to be absorbed by the body. A low blood sugar level, with symptoms of irritability and tiredness, requires the immediate intake of sugar-rich food. An excess of insulin via an injection can have serious consequences: it causes the liver to convert glucose to glycogen (a form which cannot be absorbed by body tissue), resulting in symptoms of hunger, confusion and fainting.

Vitamin supplements

These only need to be taken where there is a clear and obvious deficiency – they should not be used as an alternative to a balanced diet. All vitamins have a **recommended daily allowance (RDA)** which should not normally be exceeded, although in most cases, an excess of particular vitamins will not cause any problems. If an excess of water-soluble vitamins are digested but are not used, they are simply excreted – so vitamin C and similar tablets are usually recommended to be taken one per day. Fat-soluble vitamins can build up in the fatty tissues of the body, but the effect of this is unclear (see Concept 1, page 87).

Why you need to know these facts

All the ideas given above should be taught with the understanding that medicines are there to support the body's own systems for fighting pain and illness, or to take over where the body is deficient in particular aspects. With the increase in the number of childhood illnesses that can be treated with prescribed medicines, it is becoming much more common for medicines to be administered within the school (if not the classroom). The importance of using these medicines only as directed should be taught, both for personal safety and for the understanding of other people's needs. Children should be encouraged to understand and respect the use of medicines.

Immunization (or **vaccination**) – the act of injecting a vaccine in order to provoke the body to develop antibodies against particular infections.

Non-prescription medicines – ones which can be bought from chemists and administered by a responsible adult.

Prescription medicines – ones which are prescribed for a particular person with a particular illness, and should not be taken by anyone else.

Amazing facts

● Aspirin comes from the bark of the willow tree – before aspirin tablets were available, it was traditional to chew on willow bark for pain relief!

● In 1981, insulin became the first human hormone to be genetically engineered from bacteria.

Teaching ideas

Medical discussions (researching, questioning)
Children with specific medicinal requirements (such as asthmatics) are often very aware of their illness and have a good understanding of it. With both the child's and the parents' permission, a 'show and tell' session would probably be beneficial for all.

Research tasks (researching)
Each group of children can try to find out about a particular prescription or non-prescription medicine. Information can be obtained from a variety of sources, including books, medical advice leaflets (obtainable from chemists and doctors' surgeries), government health leaflets and multimedia encyclopaedias. In this case, Internet sources should be avoided (unless you are directed to one by a reputable source). The class may want to decide on a common set of questions first and record their findings in a standard format. The children could write letters of enquiry, or send e-mails to reputable suppliers of this kind of information (government agencies or drug companies).

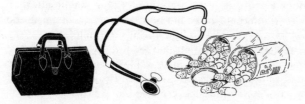

Concept 5: Drug misuse

Subject facts

Addictive prescription medicines

There is a range of prescription medicines that may be
appropriately prescribed to treat specific medical conditions
but have the potential, due to their addictive nature, to lead
to additional problems. Withdrawal symptoms after using
such medicines are not uncommon. There have been
notable cases in the recent past where patients have
become addicted to anti-depressants and tranquillizers such
as Prozac, Librium and Valium. These are normally
prescribed only to adults and for short periods of time, so
any potential addiction will probably be that of the adult;
however, an addiction may have secondary effects on
children in the household. **Analgesics**, which are
prescribed for serious pain relief, have forms that are
addictive and can be closely related to illegal narcotic forms
of the drug – in fact, some prescription drugs (such as
morphine) are illegal if held for non-medicinal purposes.

Tobacco

This is a legal, but highly addictive and toxic drug. The
addictive element, **nicotine**, affects blood pressure to
produce a calming sensation. Inhaling the smoke allows
toxic, carcinogenic gases to enter the lungs. The tar in the
smoke blocks the alveoli in the lungs, reducing the
effectiveness of respiration and leading to breathing
problems (see Chapter 3, page 42). The carbon monoxide
content in the smoke reduces the ability of the blood to
carry oxygen, leading to increased blood pressure and

consequent heart problems. The capacity of arteries is reduced, leading to poor blood supply in the extremities of the body – in extreme cases necessitating the amputation of limbs. Further carcinogens attack the lungs, throat, mouth and stomach, causing tumours which are usually fatal. **Passive smoking** (inhaling 'second-hand' smoke) can also result in the development of cancers.

Alcohol

Alcohol can become physically addictive in large doses. It affects the nervous system as a mild anaesthetic (painkiller), aiding relaxation and slowing muscular reactions. Larger amounts can seriously affect overall motor control (speech and movement), ultimately leading to unconsciousness, coma and potentially death. Over long periods of time, persistent alcohol abuse can cause liver and brain damage, resulting in death. Most alcohol-related injury and sudden death is the result of using machinery or driving while under the influence. There are significant links between the use of alcohol and outbursts of violent and irrational behaviour.

Solvents

Inhaling fumes from **solvents** (glue, cleaning fluids, butane gas, white spirit and so on) causes an intoxicated state. It can seriously affect behaviour, resulting in hallucinations and loss of control over bodily functions. There can be immediate and irreparable damage to the lungs, liver and brain. Most of the deaths from solvent abuse are a result of inhaling vomit while unconscious.

Illegal addictive drugs

The range of illegally available drugs are described and discussed in very clear terms in a variety of pamphlets and booklets available from your local health education office or LEA. Space here does not permit adequate coverage of this delicate area.

Ethical issues

In any classroom discussion of drug problems, there are real ethical issues that need careful handling, especially if someone in the family is a drug user (for example, a smoker). It is important to stress that it is the behaviour, not the person, that is the problem. Awareness that some forms of drug use are more socially acceptable than others is relevant – but the dangers of legal and even prescribed drugs must not be ignored.

All drugs, especially when taken inappropriately, have the ability to do harm to the human body – including prescribed and 'over the counter' medicines. The use of non-medicinal or 'recreational' drugs is generally seen as a problem that can be addressed through preventative education. However, the issues need to be discussed in the context of wider social circumstances that go beyond the scope of classroom science.

Vocabulary

Drug – any chemical that enters and has an effect on the body.
Addiction – a physical craving for a substance, which can lead to 'withdrawal symptoms'.
Tobacco – a highly addictive, carcinogenic substance made from the leaves of the tobacco plant, and containing the drug nicotine.

Amazing facts

● Among new cases of lung cancer, 90% are tobacco addicts – and 90% of these will die as a direct result of the cancer.
● At current (2000) prices, a 20 cigarettes per day habit will cost £1300 per year or £32 500 over a 25-year period.
● Each year, 3000 adults in the USA die as a result of passive smoking.

Common misconceptions

Alcohol is not dangerous if consumed in small amounts.
Although it may not be directly harmful to the user, any use of the drug impairs judgement and may lead to rash and dangerous acts, such as physical violence or driving a car with impaired reactions. The legal limit for blood alcohol level in a driver is below that needed to be 'drunk'.

Low tar cigarettes are less harmful.
Any intake of carcinogenic chemicals is harmful and potentially lethal. Even passive smoking can cause health problems such as asthma in children, and can lead to untreatable damage later in life. Individuals react to these toxic substances differently: one person who smokes high tar cigarettes may survive for longer than someone else who smokes a low tar brand. Many other factors, such as the effectiveness of filters, how much of the cigarette is smoked and how deeply it is inhaled, have to be taken into account.

Smoking can be used as a slimming aid.
In so far as sucking on a cigarette is an alternative oral
activity to eating, then yes. Other, equally health-damaging
options for losing weight would be to 'fill up' on polystyrene
beads, to staple your lips together or to have a limb
surgically removed. Smoking tobacco does depress the
appetite slightly – mainly because it damages the taste buds
and makes eating a less pleasant experience. In overall
health terms, there are far more effective and less
damaging options for weight reduction – such as regular
exercise and sensible diet.

Purely scientific questions about drugs are the easy ones!
But teaching about drugs and their harmful effects is bound
to lead to more difficult questions: 'Why does my Mum
smoke if she knows it will kill her?', 'Why does Dad hit me
when he's been drinking?' Your school, as a whole, needs to
prepare to deal positively with questions like these, and to
involve other support services and parents when
appropriate. As with sex education, it is worth involving
parents in the forward planning and arranging to provide
support for them where they request it. Often, educating the
child means educating the whole family.

Questions

What makes drugs addictive?
Addiction is a continued physical need for a drug. Through
taking a drug, your body can build up a tolerance to its
effect, requiring larger and larger intakes to have the same
effect. An actual addiction is when the body physically
needs the drug to maintain a balance and will become 'ill' if
the drug is withdrawn (headaches, nausea and
sleeplessness are common drug 'withdrawal symptoms').
Drug taking can also be 'habit forming': people get used to
doing it because it makes them feel happier or more
confident, and so find it hard to give up even though there is
no physical addiction.

Why are some alcoholic drinks stronger than others?
Alcohol-based drinks are not pure alcohol: they are a mix of
alcohol, water and various flavourings. The higher the
alcohol content, the 'stronger' the drink. Beers, wines and
spirits are made by different chemical processes, which
produce different concentrations of alcohol. There are
natural limits to the strength of alcoholic drinks produced
by fermentation alone: an unusually strong home-made
wine will contain highly toxic 'long-chain' alcohols.

Smoking machine (modelling, observing)

The model shown in Figure 1 can be used with small groups to demonstrate the more obvious effects on the lungs of inhaling tobacco smoke. The smoke is 'inhaled' through the cotton wool in a 'pooter' (see Chapter 6, page 146) by drawing back the plunger in a syringe. 'Inhale' with your finger on the hole in the syringe, then 'exhale' with the finger off to let the smoke escape. Once the cigarette has been smoked, examine the cotton wool: it will now be yellow and sticky from the tar in the tobacco smoke. Go on to discuss other problems of smoking such as the smell, personal hygiene problems and reduced ability to taste.

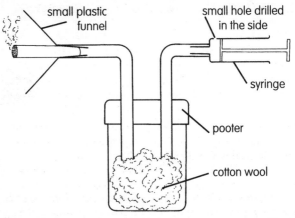

small plastic funnel

small hole drilled in the side

syringe

pooter

cotton wool

Figure 1

Resources

The following will be useful for classroom work (perhaps extending to the hall or gym) on the human body and health-related topics:
● magazines or catalogues containing photos of different-aged people from a range of ethnic groups
● stop-watches (for work on the heart rate)
● breakfast cereal packets (plus any other packages containing nutrition panels)
● a computer spreadsheet
● Government publications about drugs, health and diet
● information sheets from drug companies.

Chapter 5
GREEN PLANTS

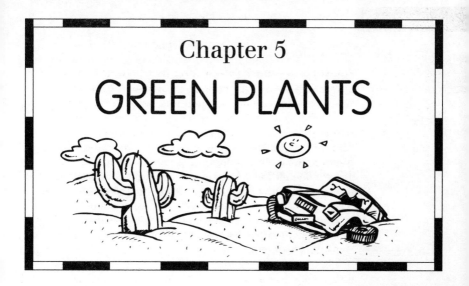

Green plants are the primary producers of energy in most ecosystems. As such, they are one of the most crucial life forms on this planet. They are also one of the most diverse and noticeable forms of organism in most of the environments that children are likely to be familiar with. Given their nature, small plants are also acceptable as subjects for experimentation. The key ideas to be developed here are:

1. Plants require certain conditions to be able to photosynthesize, which provides them with energy for nutrition and growth.
2. Reproduction in flowering plants occurs through the pollination and fertilization of seeds.
3. Reproduction in non-flowering plants can occur in other ways.

Green plants concept chain
For general comments on concept chains, see page 10.

KS1
Plants need light, warmth and water to grow. Different plants require different amounts of light, warmth and water to grow best. Plants have different parts, which perform different functions. Flowering plants produce seeds in their

flower heads; under the correct conditions, these seeds can grow into new plants. Some plants do not grow from seeds, but can grow from cuttings or bulbs. The size of the seed does not give any indication of the size of the adult plant. Seeds can be stored before planting.

KS2

The rate of plant growth depends on the availability of light, warmth and water. Different plants require different growing conditions. All green plants are dependent on light to produce food. Food is produced in the leaves of a green plant. Roots provide an anchor for a plant, and collect moisture. Plants have internal veins which transport moisture and nutrients around the plant. Flowering plants reproduce through a cycle of pollination, fertilization, seed dispersal and germination. Different seeds germinate under different conditions. Seeds contain enough food for the new plant to grow and develop until it is able to make food for itself.

KS3

Green plants obtain carbon by photosynthesizing complex carbon molecules from the carbon dioxide found in air. The mass of a plant comes from the combination of carbon with water to produce carbohydrate. Plants use oxygen (respiration) to convert the carbohydrate into cellulose (tough structural fibres) or starch (a food store), releasing some carbon dioxide back into the atmosphere. Each type of plant has an ideal level of light, warmth and carbon dioxide for maximizing photosynthesis. The structure of a plant cell is such that when it is engorged with water (turgid), it is relatively rigid. Flowering plants (and non-flowering, seed-bearing plants) contain both male and female elements, which combine in reproduction.

Concept 1: Plant growth

Subject facts

Photosynthesis

Green plants are solar-powered machines. They have the ability to use the energy in sunlight to build **carbohydrates** – the food source used, either directly or indirectly, by every animal on the planet. This process is called **photosynthesis**,

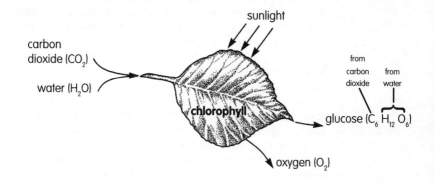

Figure 1

and is also performed by some algae and bacteria.

Photosynthesis is a chemical process (see Figure 1) in which energy (sunlight) is used to convert two common substances, **carbon dioxide** and **water,** into two different substances: **glucose** (a simple sugar) and **oxygen.** The same chemicals that enter the process come out the other end, but they are arranged differently. This reaction does not occur spontaneously whenever carbon dioxide and water happen to meet on a sunny day: it requires a chemical **catalyst** to make it happen. The catalyst is **chlorophyll**, a pigment which gives leaves their green colour. This substance absorbs light energy and uses it to drive the chemical conversion.

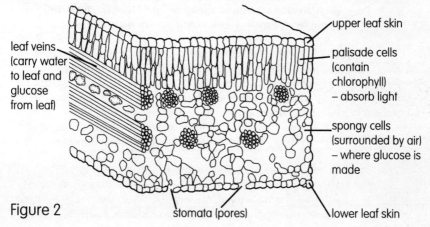

Figure 2

The by-product of the process, oxygen, is released back into the atmosphere, while the glucose is retained within the plant. Figure 2 shows a cross-section of a leaf. Vessels (similar to those which bring water to the leaf) take the glucose solution to the rest of the plant, where it is used as an energy source to build leaves, flowers, fruit and seeds. Some glucose is converted to other forms of carbohydrate: **cellulose** (to give cell walls their structure) or **starch** (a means of storing the energy). Stored energy is mainly contained in the root system, the leaves, the seeds or fruits around the seeds – these are the most nutritious parts of the plant, as far as most animals are concerned. Some animals, such as the cow, are also able to derive energy by breaking down cellulose. The glucose used to build fruits provides their sweet taste and energy content.

Rates of photosynthesis

Enzymes (biological catalysts) within the plant control the rate of photosynthesis. There are several factors which affect the rate at which green plants are able to convert carbon dioxide and water into oxygen and glucose, the main ones being the availability of carbon dioxide, light and water and the temperature:

● When the amount of carbon dioxide in the atmosphere is increased, the rate of photosynthesis (for a given level of light) increases until the enzymes are not able to work any faster. This means that as levels of atmospheric carbon dioxide rise, so does the rate at which plants convert it into glucose and oxygen.

● The brighter the sunlight, the greater the rate of photosynthesis – up to the maximum that the enzymes are capable of. Beyond that, there is very little effect.

● There is an optimum temperature for photosynthesis. Different plants have evolved different optimum temperatures to match their environment: desert plants have a higher optimum than, say, pine trees that grow in the north of Scotland. Neither would grow particularly well if they swapped places. Both above and below the optimum temperature, the rate of photosynthesis will decrease.

● There is also an optimum level of soil moisture. This level depends on the type of plant: water lilies prefer a damper soil than cacti, for example. Too much water will engorge the plant cells and cause them to burst. Water use is also dependent on other factors, such as the temperature and the rate of photosynthesis. Plants **transpire** (release water by evaporation from their leaf surfaces) in order to draw more water (containing dissolved mineral nutrients) into the plant through the roots. The rate of **transpiration** (like perspiration in animals) increases with temperature. The need for water itself increases with the rate of photosynthesis, since water is a vital part of the photosynthetic process (carbon extracted from carbon dioxide is combined with water to make carbohydrate) and is also needed to transport the products of photosynthesis from the leaf cells to the rest of the plant.

Vegetable protein

As animals require protein for growth (see Chapter 4, page 84), so do plants. Seeds (particularly grains and beans) are particularly rich in protein, due to their role as food stores for growth in the life cycle of the plant. Plants are not able to ingest proteins: they have to make them from basic chemicals. Glucose provides most of the chemicals, but nitrogen, phosphates and potassium are also required. Most plants usually extract these from the soil.

● **Nitrogen** is necessary to make the proteins used in cell membranes, DNA, enzymes and chlorophyll. Plants lacking sufficient nitrogen have yellowing leaves and stunted growth. Some plants, living in regions where the soil nitrogen level is particularly poor, have evolved into 'carnivores': they trap insects and other small animals to ingest their nitrogen.

● A **potassium**-deficient plant will produce new leaves that are yellow, due to the lack of a particular enzyme that is important in the control of photosynthesis.

● Insufficient **phosphate** will result in a plant having stunted root growth and new leaves that are purple-tinged, again due to an inability to synthesize necessary enzymes.

At Key Stages 1 and 2, a difficult line must be walked. Children are expected to understand the conditions that plants require for healthy growth without being given an explanation of photosynthesis, the key process responsible for growth. They receive information from many sources concerning the importance of plants in the production of oxygen, which all animals need in order to breathe. They

Why you need to know these facts

are constantly being warned of the dangers of cutting down rainforests and the over-production of carbon dioxide through car exhausts and industry. But **why** do plants produce oxygen? Children need to realize that it is a by-product of a process that leads to plant growth. An understanding of the other factors that lead to plant growth will enable them to gain a better appreciation of the crucial role that plants play in the environment (see Chapter 7).

Vocabulary

Photosynthesis – the process by which light energy is used to convert carbon dioxide and water into glucose and oxygen.
Chlorophyll – the chemical that makes the photosynthesis process work.
Catalyst – a substance that enables a chemical reaction to take place.
Transpiration – water loss from plant leaves, causing more water to be drawn up through the roots.

Amazing facts

● Every year, photosynthesizing organisms produce about 170 billion tonnes of new carbohydrates. That's about 30 tonnes for every person on Earth – but of course, we do have to share it with other animals!
● The largest known leaf belongs to the Amazonian bamboo palm. It is 20 metres long.

Common misconceptions

Wood is made from the soil.
This is a common mistake; it seems to arise from a difficulty in understanding that a solid (cellulose) can be made by combining a liquid (water) with a gas (carbon dioxide). The child assumes that the solid must have had its origin in another solid medium: the soil. This belief shows that the child has not fully understood the effects of photosynthesis.

More water means a bigger plant.
This is an almost inevitable conclusion of poorly managed 'with and without' science experiments from the primary school of years gone by. No water and the plant dies; provide water and it lives – from which children were often left to infer that the more water a plant has, the better it grows! More effective experiments would show that there is an optimum level of soil moisture for the growth of any given plant. Children need to be aware that over-watering a pot plant can damage it.

Plants give off carbon dioxide at night.

Plants give off carbon dioxide all the time: they need oxygen to **respire**, converting the food they have made into usable energy. (There are similarities with animal respiration here – see Chapter 3, page 53.) The waste product of this respiration is carbon dioxide. During the day, when plants are photosynthesizing, they are using up more carbon dioxide than they are producing through respiration; there is thus a net increase in the oxygen level in the air around them. At night, when no photosynthesis is taking place but the plant is still respiring, there is a net increase in carbon dioxide and a reduction in the oxygen level around them. For this reason, it used to be common practice to remove pot plants (and even cut flowers) from hospital wards at nightfall for the patients' benefit.

Why are plants green?

Questions

Because that's the colour of the chlorophyll in the leaves and stalks. It also has some important implications for photosynthesis. Plants appear green because green light is reflected from them. As photosynthesis works on the light absorbed into cells, the colour of this light must be a mixture of red and blue. A plant grown under green light will reflect rather than absorb the light energy, and so will not be able to photosynthesize. Note that the colour of natural light from the sky may be red or blue, but is never green!

Basic tips about plant investigations

Teaching ideas

● Avoid binary 'with and without' experiments: they are an oversimplification and can lead to inappropriate findings.
● Avoid having one plant per child: nobody wants 'their' plant to die, so fair tests may not be fairly conducted! Few children will be particularly happy about being placed in charge of the plant that will not be receiving any water as part of an investigation into the water requirements of plants, and may end up cheating to protect their plant.
● If you want to grow plants for the children to take home at the end of term, do this separately from fair tests.
● Use more than one plant in each 'condition' when testing: repetition makes the test more accurate.
● Plant growth provides opportunities for a range of related investigations to be carried out by groups, as in the examples below.

Growing plants – light (planning, testing, recording)

Different groups can address different aspects of plant growth: colour of light ('glass houses' made from different-coloured plastic drinks bottles); light intensity (wattage of bulb); duration (hours per day the plant is exposed to the light); frequency (number of times the light goes on and off in a day). They should use the same type of plants under the same conditions over a number of weeks, and record the changes using a video or other camera or by direct measurements (recorded on a computer spreadsheet). Each group can present their findings to the others.

Growing plants – water 1 (planning, testing, recording)

Do all plants need the same amount of water? The children can try giving plants of different types (but of roughly the same size) the same amount of water to see the effect. (Avoid spiny cacti or other potentially dangerous plants.)

Growing plants – water 2 (planning, testing, recording)

How does watering affect growth? Using the same type of plants, different groups can try altering: the amount of water given; the frequency of watering (for example, 500ml once a week or 100ml per day); the time of watering (morning, noon or afternoon); the method of watering (in the pot, on the leaves); the type of water given (tap, distilled, salty); the temperature of the water. Each group should record its results. The activity could be repeated for different types of plant and the results compared.

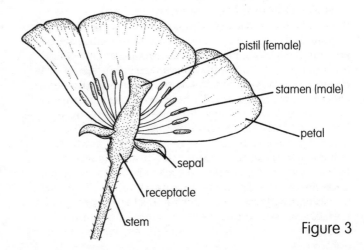

Figure 3

Figure 4

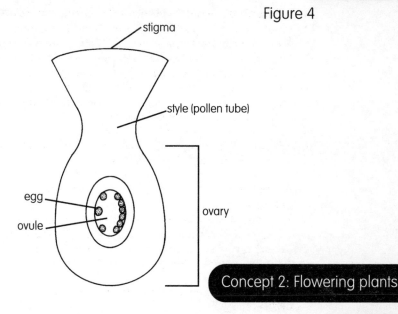

stigma

style (pollen tube)

egg

ovule

ovary

Flower parts

Although the flower heads of different plants vary, most
have recognizably similar parts. The first part of the flower
to grow on the end of a specialized flower stem is the
receptacle, from which all of the other flower parts
eventually grow. A covering called the **sepal**, which splits to
let the flower out when it is ready, protects the flower **bud**.
The flower **petals** are designed to attract insects or other
small animals by their colour or smell.

Working inwards from the sepal (see Figure 3), there are
the petals, the **stamen** (male organ) and the **pistil** (female
organ). Those flowers that most closely resemble their
ancient ancestors, such as the buttercup, have this basic
format, whereas flowers that have developed more recently
can be very different. The daisy, for example, is a compact
cluster of many minute flowers crammed together on one
head. Some plants produce separate male and female
flowers (such as grapevines and oak trees); some even have
separate male and female plants (such as willow trees).

The pistil (also called the **carpel** in some books) has a
sticky opening at the top, called the **stigma**, to which pollen
grains become attached (see Figure 4). Below the stigma is
the **style**, which contains the **pollen tube** that the sperms
(usually two per pollen grain) travel along to reach the
ovary, where the **ovule** that contains the eggs can be found.

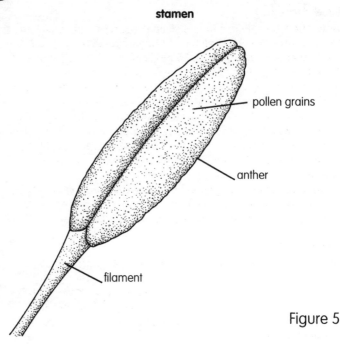

stamen

pollen grains

anther

filament

Figure 5

The male part of the flower consists of a thin stalk called a **filament**, topped by an **anther** in which the **pollen** grows until it is released on reaching maturity (see Figure 5).

Pollination

Some flowers are **self-pollinating**, which means that the pollen from the anther can fertilize eggs in the ovary of the same flower. However, most flowers are **cross-pollinating** and rely on the wind, water or an animal to carry the pollen produced in one flower to the stigma of another flower of the same species. Flowering plants evolved long after animals appeared on land, and many have developed a relationship of mutual dependence with a particular species of animal.

When it reaches the stigma, the pollen grain will break to release the sperm, one of which will fertilize the egg contained in the ovary. An ovary may contain just one or many eggs, depending on the type of plant.

Fertilization

Once the egg is fertilized, the ovule surrounding it will harden to provide a protective seed shell. The ovary might expand to form a fleshy fruit (apple, cherry), a dry fruit (almond, hazelnut) or a grain (wheat, rice).

Seed dispersal

To further the species, plants must **disperse** their fertilized seeds in order to colonize new habitats and give each seed the best chance of survival. By covering them in a fleshy **fruit**, the plant encourages larger animals to eat them and then, later, to excrete the seeds further away. Dandelion and sycamore seeds, with their 'parachute' and 'wing' structures, are excellent examples of dispersal by wind. The coconut, which grows by the sea, has a large seed that will float to another location to grow. The teasel has a 'fruit' that is covered in hooks and will become securely attached to mammal fur (or human clothing).

None of these dispersal systems are particularly effective, and plants have to produce many seeds to make it likely that some of them will find somewhere suitable to grow.

Germination

On finding a place where the conditions are appropriate (sufficient amounts of water, warmth and oxygen – light may also be a factor), a seed will **germinate** and begin to grow into a new plant. This might be after a considerable period of **dormancy** – but as time goes by, the viability of the seed decreases.

In germination, water is absorbed by the seed, causing the embryo inside to expand and split the casing. The embryo now has access to oxygen, which allows the energy stored within the seed to be utilized for growth. The **radicle** (root) is the first part of the seedling to emerge, followed by the **hypocotyl** (shoot), to which the **plumule** (rudimentary leaves) are attached.

Once the hypocotyl has reached the surface of the soil and is receiving light, photosynthesis can begin and the seedling no longer has to rely on the store of energy in the seed. If the seed is buried too deep or is in too dark a place to begin photosynthesizing before its store of energy is depleted, it will die.

Flowering cycles

Some flowering plants (particularly those in desert regions) have irregular flowering cycles based on the availability of water. After lying dormant for months or even years, these plants will spring into action when it finally rains and go through their flowering cycle before it becomes dry once more. Other flowering plants in tropical conditions, where there are no seasonal variations and the growing conditions are ideal the whole year round, may be constantly in flower or may only flower once in every few years.

Most flowering plants progress through a life cycle whose stages are broadly similar to those described above. In order to understand gardening and horticulture, the children need to know about the plant's sexual organs and the parts that they play in the reproductive cycle, and how to identify them in various species.

Vocabulary

Pistil – the female part of the flower, containing the **stigma**, **style** and **ovary**.

Ovule – the part of the ovary that contains the egg.

Stamen – the male part of the flower, comprising the **anther** and **filament**.

Pollen – the granule that delivers the male genetic material to the female seed.

Pollination – the process by which the pollen reaches the stigma.

Fertilization – the point at which the sperm from the pollen meets the egg in the ovary.

Dormant – when growth is suspended at a very low level of metabolism.

Germination – the point at which the dormant embryo begins to grow into a seedling.

Amazing facts

● The 'stinking corpse lily' produces a flower (no prizes for guessing the scent) that is 1m across, with each petal growing up to 45cm in length. The largest natural British bloom, the white water lily, is only 15cm wide.

● The smallest flower (1mm in diameter) belongs to an orchid.

● The 'double coconut' tree produces a fruit weighing 18kg.

● A flowering herb found in the Bolivian Andes flowers only once in its lifetime, after 80–150 years of growth.

Common misconceptions

Old seeds won't grow.
It depends on how they have been stored. Older seeds tend to be less viable (a smaller proportion will germinate), but some will still grow if they have been stored correctly (in dry, cool, dark conditions). An Arctic lupin seed found frozen in Canada was thawed out and grown – and that was approximately 15 000 years old! There have been several reports of seeds found in Egyptian pyramids germinating successfully after thousands of years.

Why don't flowers just pollinate themselves?
Most flowers are able to self-pollinate, but cross-pollination results in the sharing of genetic material, which means that the new plant will be slightly different from its parents. This increases **variation** and so gives the plant species a greater chance of long-term survival (see page 152).

Flower dissection (observing, recording)
Children can work in small groups to observe different flowers, noting similarities and differences. They can cut open the flower heads with sharp knives **(on cutting boards, with careful supervision)** to reveal the ovary and other parts, then fix them to a sheet of paper with double-sided sticky tape and label them.

Flower walk (observing, sorting)
Take a group of children for a walk through a flower garden or wild flower meadow (or even a garden centre). Ask them to observe and draw some of the different flower heads, then attempt to sort them into their own different groups. **(NB Be aware of any children who are allergic to pollen and take action accordingly.)**

Bean dissection (observing, recording)
Soften runner or broad beans by soaking them in water. Ask the children to draw what they think might be inside; discuss their ideas. Cut open some beans (using a sharp knife) and ask the children to draw what they observe. Discuss how what they can see compares with their original ideas.

Germination (observing, recording)
A group of children can soak some beans and place them on a sheet of damp kitchen paper, with a further damp sheet over them. They should keep the beans somewhere dark and return to observe them on a daily basis, recording changes. Remind them to keep the beans damp – but not to drown them!

Grow a plant (observing, planning)
Working in groups, children can follow the instructions on seed packets and grow plants from seeds. They should keep a diary of the changes. (NB Choose the species carefully to ensure that the seeds are of a manageable size and beware of seeds covered in chemicals.)

Flowering plant reproduction – without flowers

Even flowering plants don't always need to use flowers to make more of themselves. There are several other methods: **bulbs** (daffodils, tulips), **tubers** (potatoes), **corm** (croci), **trailing plants** (spider plants, strawberries), and **cuttings** (geraniums). Each of these methods produces a genetically identical copy of the original plant.

Conifers

Conifer trees and shrubs avoid the need for flowers altogether. This form of plant life developed long before the flowering plants, and is still going strong. Like flowering plants, conifers produce seeds that (once fertilized) contain an embryonic plant and a store of food. These seeds are not produced within an ovary, however. Conifers are defined by their production of **cones** – woody fruits within which the seeds develop. A cone, which can take a few years to form, produces a seed at the base of each of its 'fingers'. When these seeds mature, and the weather conditions are favourable, the cone will open up and allow the wind to disperse the seeds.

Pines, a sub-group of the conifers, produce two types of cone: male and female. The male cones, which are relatively small, develop on the lower branches in groups of up to 50. They mature in late spring, releasing their pollen into the wind, then shrivel up and drop off. The female cones grow higher up in the same trees, singularly or in small groups, and are about five times the size of the male cones. The pollen from the male cones is blown upwards by the wind and into the female cones.

Once the seeds are fertilized, the female cones close up to let the seeds develop; this can take up to three years. In this time, the cone becomes woodier as it turns from green to brown. Once they are mature, the seeds are released into the wind to be dispersed. Alternatively, small animals may break open the cones and take the seeds, eating some and storing the rest. Often the animal will not return to its store of seeds, giving them the opportunity to grow.

Children need to realize that flowers are not always necessary for plants to reproduce. Even some flowering plants do not need to reproduce from flowers. This knowledge will help them to understand how our food is grown, and how pine trees have survived in cold climates.

Cone – a woody 'fruit' with scales that protect the seeds.
Conifer – a cone-bearing tree or shrub.
Bulb – a swollen, layered stem base from which regrowth is possible.
Tuber – a swollen root from which regrowth is possible.

Amazing facts

● The Great Basin Bristlecone pines in the USA are the oldest living things on the planet. Some of these trees are over 5000 years old.
● 39 members of a family of pine trees that was thought to have been extinct for 50 million years were discovered not far from Sydney in 1994.

Common misconceptions

Conifers only grow in cold countries.
Yes, some do. But there are other types of conifer that grow in hot, dry countries. The cedar grows in the Middle East, North Africa and Northern India – often in hot, dry, mountainous regions where its cones protect the seeds from damage due to heat and lack of water.

Teaching ideas

Cone collection (observing, sorting)
Ask the children to collect cones from forest floors when they are on holiday or out walking. **NB They should only take cones that have fallen to the ground.** In the classroom, compare some of the cones together. The children can break open some common types of cone to discover the seeds, and try to work out what type of tree each cone came from.

Cut and run (testing, observing)
Ask the children to talk to their parents about taking small cuttings from plants in their home or garden to grow at school. Which plants grow most easily from cuttings? (Most good gardening books will provide full details on the use of cuttings.) The most important thing to remember is to suspend the end of the cutting in water; poking it through cling film stretched over a container of water is an effective method. The children could also talk to their parents about plants with runners (creeping stems that can take root separately from the main plant) in the garden – strawberries are a common example.

Resources

You should provide a range of examples of plants, seeds and flowers for the children to examine. Refer to the ASE booklet *Be Safe!* (available from ASE Publications) to avoid the dangerous ones.

For investigative activities, you will need plant growing materials: a growing medium, pots, watering devices, light sources, timing devices and several plastic drinks bottles of various colours (to make 'glass houses').

For germination activities, please don't fall back on cress: it's over-familiar and boring! Sweet peas are quite easy to grow, and the size of the seed makes for easy handling. Radish seeds are also worth trying. With all seeds, you should wash them to make sure that they are safe to touch – they often come coated with anti-fungal chemicals.

Video and still cameras will be useful for recording results, and a computer spreadsheet program will help the children to present measurements made under different conditions over a period of time.

The BBC video *Life of Plants* provides useful background knowledge for classroom work on this subject.

Chapter 6
MINIBEASTS

Although the term 'invertebrate' has no real scientific validity, it is useful for collecting together all of those animals that do not have a spinal nerve cord. 'Minibeasts' could be used as a more familiar alternative – it is equally invalid in scientific terms. While some marine and tropical 'invertebrates' are fairly huge, those that the children will encounter in Britain can reasonably be described as 'minibeasts'.

The great diversity of these animals provides opportunities for children to practise observing and classifying. Because of their size, habitat and food needs, there is quite a range of such creatures that can be kept safely in captivity in an appropriate environment without any undue ethical concerns. (See the ASE booklet *Be Safe!* for a list of suitable animals.) Most have fairly brief life cycles, and many go through remarkable changes in form. The key ideas to be developed are:

1. Animals can be classified by their observable similarities and differences through the use of sorting keys.

2. The life cycles of many of these animals, particularly arthropods, exhibit significant metamorphic developments.

3. Observation and collection must be carried out with due care and consideration, and with appropriate techniques and tools.

Invertebrate concept chain

For general comments on concept chains, see page 10.

KS1

Many different minibeasts inhabit the local environment.
Different minibeasts can be found in different places.
Minibeasts can be sorted and grouped according to their
observable features. Careful collection, storage and
handling is necessary for closer observation. Some
minibeasts progress through significantly different stages in
their life cycle.

KS2

The key features of a minibeast can be linked to the habitat
in which it lives. Sorting keys can be produced and used to
sort and identify particular species. The young and adult
forms of a particular species of minibeast may look very
different. When a minibeast is kept in captivity, the habitat
and food that it needs must be provided; as with any living
thing, proper care must be taken of it.

KS3

Minibeasts perform a wide range of roles within an
ecosystem. Categorization is based on observable features,
some of which may only be seen in the natural habitat. A
metamorphosis divides particular phases within the life
cycle of a minibeast, each one demonstrating a significantly
different lifestyle.

Concept 1: Sorting keys

Subject facts

Whenever a child drags some poor unsuspecting minibeast
out from under a stone (or from a pond) and thrusts it
under your nose for closer inspection, you will invariably be
asked a version of 'What's this called?' Usually, the
instinctive response is to tell the child, so that he or she will
take it away! Try to resist. Let the words 'I'm not sure – but I
know how to find out!' burst forth instead – you'll feel better
for it in the end. If you want to be seen as the world
authority on minibeasts, fine; but helping the children to
find out for themselves is both the most effective long-term
solution and the most scientifically useful.

Encourage the children to observe the minibeast closely (the sense of sight is quite enough!) and identify its main features. Suggest looking for features that are easy to identify:

● *How many legs does it have?* (None, six, eight, many.)
● *Does it have wings?* (No, one pair, two pairs.)
● *How many body segments does it have?* (One, two, three, many.)
● *Does it have a hard body shell?* (Yes, no.)

Even these four questions will move the child a long way towards classifying the minibeast in question. For example, if it has no legs, no wings, no body shell and one body segment, it is probably a slug. For other combinations of answers, there will be many possible candidates – think how many different types of fly, spider or beetle there are. For such minibeasts, a reference book will be needed (see Resources on page 149).

In addition to close visual observation of the minibeast, another important factor in categorization is where it was found – assuming that it was found in its natural habitat (for example, house flies that have been found on the surface of a pond). Pond life, in particular, provides ample opportunity for observation and sorting; the *Observer's Book of Pond Life* (Warne) contains an excellent sorting key on its front and back inside covers.

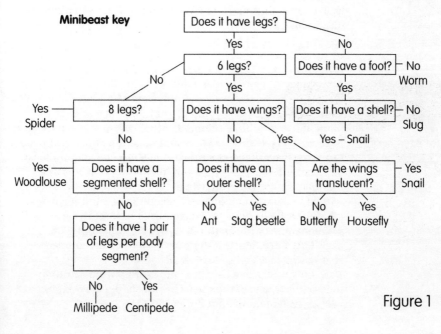

Figure 1

Minibeasts

Why you need to know these facts

Being able to sort and classify using observable similarities and differences is a key skill within science curricula. It is particularly emphasized in biology, and working with locally found minibeasts in their natural habitat provides children with the opportunity to work with live specimens, developing appropriate techniques and attitudes. Children should be able to use and make sorting diagrams or sorting keys of the type shown in Figure 1 (see page 139).

Vocabulary

Key – a questioning device that allows the progressive narrowing down of the classification of an unknown living thing (or object) based on its observable or testable features.

Body segments – the number of clearly defined sections a minibeast has, including the head and/or tail. An insect has three body segments, an arachnid two.

Amazing facts

● There are at least 800 000 species of insect that have been identified.
● Millipedes range in length from 2mm to 29cm long, and have between 36 and 750 legs.
● Some midges beat their wings at over 1000 beats per second.
● The buzzing sounds of flying insects (flies, wasps and so on) are made by their wings.

Common misconceptions

Caterpillars, millipedes and centipedes are all the same. At a glance, they may look similar: living tubes with a lot of legs. However, they are quite different. Millipedes and centipedes are closely related, but millipedes have two pairs of legs per body segment, while centipedes have one pair per body segment. The walking action of the millipede is almost wave-like, while that of a centipede is more jerky and beetle-like. Caterpillars are not adult creatures at all, but the infant form or **larvae** of butterflies or moths that will later undergo metamorphosis into the adult form. Not all of their body segments have legs: the front three segments have true (jointed) legs, and some of the tail segments have jointless pegs or 'prolegs'. The middle sections often have no legs at all.

In fact, the closer you look, the more obviously different these three types of minibeast are in shape, movement, eating habits and habitat.

How did they all get names?

When a newly discovered type of animal (or plant) is identified, the person who found it gets to name it. The name is usually similar to those of its nearest relatives. However, many familiar types of living thing have names that have become attached to them through common usage. There is a story that the butterfly got its name because of an accidental spoonerism when it was originally categorized several hundred years ago: the original name is reputed to have been 'flutterby', which is an altogether more apt description!

Guess who? (questioning, sorting)

This is based on the popular board game. It can be played by pairs of children, with two sets of identical cards made from pictures of various different minibeasts. Each child selects a minibeast, and has to identify the minibeast selected by his or her opponent by asking a series of categorical questions, such as 'Does it have wings?', to narrow down the field.

Alternatively, this can be played as a group or class 'Lotto' activity, with the minibeast pictures displayed on a laminated poster. The children play in two teams; each team has to guess the other team's minibeast by asking categorical questions. The children can cross off the 'wrong' minibeasts with a dry-wipe marker pen as they narrow down the field. Each team can discuss what will be the best question to ask at each stage.

Who am I? (questioning, sorting)

This is a teacher-led 'Twenty questions' approach. Think of a minibeast (one that you have a good description of, and that the children will be familiar with). Encourage the children to identify it by asking a series of questions, to which you will only answer 'yes' or 'no'. Help them to frame the questions effectively, identify redundant questions and use a 'funnelling' approach to narrow down the field (for example, don't start with 'Is it the caterpillar of a Red Admiral butterfly?').

Designing a key (questioning, sorting)

Given a few different minibeasts (either pictures or actual specimens), the children should try to think of questions that will allow them to sort and identify the minibeasts as efficiently as possible (see Figure 1 for examples). Groups

can swap keys and pictures to see how well the keys work.
Each group can then try adding an additional specimen:
how does the key need to be adapted?

Using a key (sorting, observing)
Working in groups or individually, the children can use
published keys to identify particular specimens that they
have found.

Concept 2: Metamorphosis

Subject facts

Two forms of insect metamorphosis are recognized by most
entomologists: complete and incomplete. The butterfly is an
example of a **complete metamorphosis**: the animal
progresses through an immature, larval stage before
changing, via a dormant **pupa** stage, into a mature adult
(see Figure 2). The coat protecting the pupa is commonly
known as a **cocoon**. The change from **larva** to **adult** allows
the animal to adapt to changing seasonal conditions and
make use of very different food supplies.

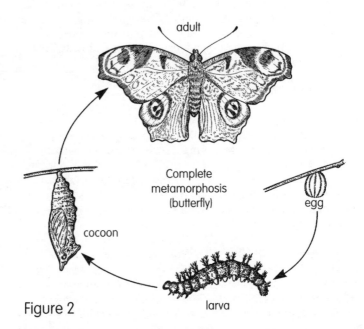

adult

Complete
metamorphosis
(butterfly)

egg

cocoon

Figure 2

larva

An **incomplete metamorphosis** is where the young and adult forms are not very different: often the immature form only lacks wings and sexual organs. In this case, the young form is called a **nymph** (see Figure 3). Again, the changes are adaptations to make use of changing habitats and food supplies. The mayfly, for example, spends one to three years as an aquatic nymph, eating and growing. Mayfly nymphs will emerge (all at the same time) from the water, shed their nymph skins and have a very short life as a winged insect – usually about 48 hours (long enough to mate). Not surprisingly, the group (or order) to which mayflies belong is called the *Ephemeroptera* (meaning 'short-lived wings').

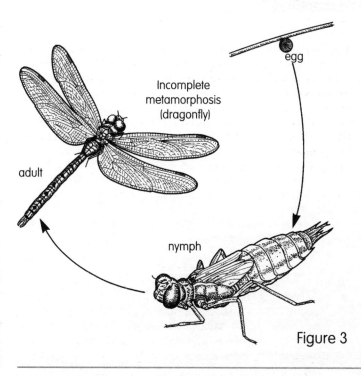

Incomplete metamorphosis (dragonfly)

egg

adult

nymph

Figure 3

Many arthropods (and insects in particular) provide excellent examples of metamorphosis: they undergo radical changes in their body structure, lifestyle and habitat as they move from one stage of their life cycle to the next. Without careful study, children are likely to assume that caterpillars and butterflies, for example, are completely different animals. The processes of insect metamorphosis can be observed over a fairly short period of time, and provide a useful introduction to the idea of biological development.

Why you need to know these facts

Minibeasts

Metamorphosis – a process of change from one form to another during a life cycle.
Larva – an immature form which bears little resemblance to the adult form.
Nymph – an immature form that bears some resemblance to the adult (the differences are usually that the adult form has wings and reproductive organs, and has a different habitat and food source).

Amazing facts

● Dragonflies shed their skins up to 20 times as nymphs where they live in ponds and streams. The nymphs can grow so large that they are able to feed on tadpoles and small fish.
● The protective covering or cocoon around a butterfly or moth pupa is spun out of a kind of silk, which is allowed to harden. Silk cloth is made from threads spun by the Silkmoth caterpillar.

Common
misconceptions

Butterflies die in the winter.
You don't see them around because of the lack of food. Many butterflies lie dormant over the winter months. A very few, such as the 'painted lady', migrate as some bird species do: in summer, they can be found as far north as Finland; in winter, they fly to southern Europe and North Africa. Relatively speaking, it is probably the most amazing migration of any animal

Questions

What is cuckoo spit?
At its larval stage, the froghopper (a type of aphid related to the greenfly) lives by sucking juice out of plants. To prevent it from drying out (and to deter predators), it surrounds itself with a froth which it produces from its anus. So the name could have been a lot worse.

Do earthworms reproduce by dividing?
No. If a small portion is cut off the head or tail, the worm can regenerate the missing portion – but the smaller part dies. Worms are **hermaphrodites** (each individual has both male and female sex organs), but the individuals usually pair up to fertilize each other. (This increases genetic variation, and is therefore good for the species.) Each individual will lay eggs, wrapped up in a cocoon, from which small, fully developed worms will emerge.

It is possible to keep some types of insect in captivity in order to observe their metamorphosis. *Be Safe!* (ASE Publications) provides a complete and very useful list of these animals. Particular species of butterfly are excellent for this purpose, as are certain cockroaches and stick insects. Eggs, along with suitable habitats and food (plants), can be obtained from butterfly farms. A class project on insect metamorphosis will allow the children to observe and record the various stages, then release the adult insects into a local environment that has been prepared with the appropriate plant life to sustain them.

Concept 3: Minibeast hunt

Subject facts

Minibeasts are found in a wide range of different habitats, and are adapted to their particular living conditions and food supplies. Awareness of this must be at the forefront of any decision to observe minibeasts in more detail by taking them out of their natural habitat for a short while. Sometimes, due to weather conditions, pupil safety or organizational factors, observations cannot be carried out on site, and capture of the minibeasts may be necessary. If this is decided to be the most appropriate option, the correct tools must be used and the children must be given guidance and training on how to use them safely and hygienically.

The children first need to know where to look. The main factors to consider are where the minibeasts will find food and shelter. Food requirements of minibeasts are quite diverse, but it is best to stick to vegetation (poking about in dead animal carcasses is **not** recommended). Vegetation could be alive (leaves, flowers) or dead (leaf litter, decaying logs) – each will provide a different range of animals. The same is true of different places where vegetation can be found: the range of animals found will depend on the moisture content of the place where the vegetation is found (particularly if it is underwater). Typical minibeasts for particular habitats are:

● Dead vegetation (logs, compost heaps) – woodlice, worms.
● Leaves – aphids, ladybirds, beetles, spiders.

● Under bushes – beetles, ants.
● On pond water – pond skaters.
● In pond water – water boatmen, caddis fly larvae, diving beetles, water fleas.

Safe collection

Always collect from somewhere unpolluted that is safe to get to and easy to oversee: take enough adult helpers to supervise all the children (mobile phones will be useful). Survey the site first, so that you know roughly where to go and what to expect; it's best to 'acclimatize' the other adults to the minibeasts as well, so that the more squeamish ones don't give off the wrong messages to the children. If you are going near water, check that it is safe to do so: avoid overhanging banks, swift-moving or deep water, or water where the edge is not clearly defined. Always ensure that the children don't put their fingers in their mouths while collecting, and that they wash their hands immediately after contact with any living thing.

Most collection devices can be made almost as easily as they can be purchased. To hunt minibeasts in bushes and low trees, little more is needed than a white sheet. Place it under the bush and shake the bush: lots of little black things appear on the sheet. The ones that start to move after 15 seconds or so are the minibeasts! To collect individual specimens (from a sheet or other places), use a white plastic teaspoon for the bigger creatures or a **pooter** (named after the sound it makes) for the smaller ones, and place them in a white margarine tub.

Figure 4 shows a typical home-made 'pooter'. A word of warning: look before you poot! By sucking on one tube, you can suck a small minibeast up the other tube into a specimen jar. It is best to use a syringe for sucking to avoid mishaps; but if you are using your mouth, be very careful not to confuse the two tubes! The tube that you suck on, which must have a piece of gauze or a grille over the end in the jar, should always be sterilized prior to use, and children should be discouraged from sharing pooters. The other tube will have been poked in some very unpleasant places in the search for minibeasts! If you mix up the two tubes, the minibeast will become stuck behind the gauze inside the wrong tube – and any other minibeasts already in the jar will end up in the back of your throat.

Pond dipping can be great fun, but you need the proper equipment. Avoid aquarium nets: they are so short that if you are near enough to the water to use one, you are probably in the water. The larger nets present two problems for children. Firstly, they are heavy, particularly when being lifted out of the water – it might be all that a child needs to topple in. Secondly, to observe the 'catch' you have to put your hand underneath and lift the net – resulting in a cascade of water down your sleeve. What I would recommend is a plastic flour sieve, with the 'ears' cut off, attached to the end of a short cane (1–1.25m). Always collect a bucket of water for the observation trays **before** the dipping starts: it will be your last chance to obtain any clear water until the sediment settles!

There are various optical instruments that can double as collection jars of various sizes; some include a mirror that allows the underside of the animal to be viewed from above. Hand lenses are very useful, but are easily lost – I would recommend the plastic type of lens with a hole in the handle for a piece of string to which the child can be attached.

With younger children, you may want to place their hands in sandwich bags to make sure that they do not touch minibeasts (or mud) directly.

Whatever you do with the minibeasts, avoid or minimize direct contact and return them to the place that they came from as quickly as possible once observation is complete. The RSPCA Code of Practice for working with minibeasts should be adhered to. Following these guidelines, I would not recommend catching any particular native species and keeping it in captivity. Captive minibeasts can be obtained from pet shops or butterfly farms.

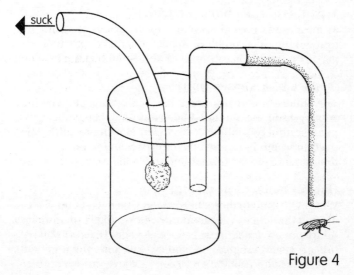

Figure 4

Why you need to know these facts

Observing minibeasts in their natural habitat is very desirable as a way of stimulating the children's environmental awareness. Study of minibeasts in greater detail needs to be guided by clear ethical considerations, and to instil in the children a sense of responsibility for the care of other forms of life.

Vocabulary

Pooter – a device for sucking smaller minibeasts into a specimen container.
Minibeast – common term for a small invertebrate.

Common misconceptions

Minibeasts are capable of tearing an adult human limb from limb.
Well, by the way some people react... Remember that children will tend to develop the same attitude towards minibeasts as you display. Try to overcome any fears that you or your helpers may have. You do not have to touch the minibeasts: indeed, you should not do so. React calmly and with consideration to these animals, and the children will do the same.

Teaching ideas

Why there? (planning, inferring)
As a class, ask the children to consider where they might find minibeasts around the school. Can they say which particular minibeasts they are likely to find, and why?

Shake a bush (observing)
The children can work in groups. Each group can place a white plastic sheet under a bush and shake the bush. How many minibeasts fall onto the sheet? How many different types are there? Is there any difference in the range of minibeasts they get from different bushes?

Habitat builder (observing)
Where it is safe to do so, help the children to set up places around the school where minibeasts are likely to be able to flourish: logs, bricks, leaf litter and so on. Over a period of time, revisit these places together to observe the minibeasts that have colonized the area.

Collection (collecting, observing)

As a class, visit different habitats to observe and collect minibeasts for more detailed observation.

Minibeast drawing (observing)

The children can use lenses to draw parts of a minibeast in fine detail.

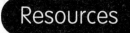

Resources

The following will all be useful for practical work involving minibeasts:
- *The Observer's Book of... Pond Life, Common Insects, Moths* and *Butterflies* (Warne)
- magni-, midi-, and minispectors
- a binocular microscope (×20 magnification)
- 1 litre margarine or ice-cream tubs
- pond dipping nets
- white plastic spoons
- aquaria
- white plastic sheets
- spreadsheet, database or branching software
- minibeast videos
- multimedia nature encyclopaedias.

Chapter 7

SHARING AND COMPETING IN THE ENVIRONMENT

Key concepts

We live in a 'closed' environment, in the sense that all living organisms on this planet rely on the success or failure of other organisms. Apart from the energy of the Sun, everything has to be recycled and used over and over again. There are many different forms of relationship between the living things that coexist on Earth: direct competition for the same space or food source; symbiotic relationships that benefit two species at once; and food relationships where both species can thrive when balanced. The 'interrelatedness' of organisms, and the way that different organisms find different niches and means of survival, will be considered here. The key ideas to be developed are:

1. An ecosystem will survive if there is a sufficient diversity of life and there is an interdependence between the members of that ecosystem.

2. Energy (or food) chains exist and continue where there are 'pyramids' of numbers or biomass: primary producers (such as green plants) supporting successively smaller numbers of organisms at each level of the pyramid.

3. Each living organism is adapted to fulfil a particular role within a particular ecological niche.

Environment concept chain

For general comments on concept chains, see page 10.

KS1

Many different plants and animals coexist in the local environment. There are many different environments. Different environments support different plants and animals. Different plants and animals are suited to different environments. What particular animals are present in a particular environment depends on the availability of food.

KS2

Animals and plants are adapted to the environments in which they can be found. An environment consists of a number of factors, including the terrain, and the availability of water, heat, light and nutrition. Changes to the environment will require that the living things either adapt or relocate to survive. Seasonal environmental changes often result in behavioural adaptation, physical change, migration or a period of dormancy for the organisms living there. There are feeding relationships in every ecosystem that can be traced from primary producer to higher predator. Energy cycles can be completed by decomposers (such as fungi and some micro-organisms) that return important chemicals to the soil. The environment in which an organism can be found can be deduced from a study of the organism's features.

KS3

The population of an organism within an environment depends on how successfully it competes for food and space with other organisms occupying the same niche. Humans have a significant effect on the environment, causing many changes. A foreign organism introduced to a closed environment will cause changes in the numbers of other organisms. Artificial environments may be used to farm particular species of plant or animal. Green plants produce energy in a form that can be consumed by other organisms, particularly animals. The chemical building blocks of living things, such as carbon and nitrogen, require constant recycling within an ecosystem.

An **ecosystem** is the combination of a **habitat** (a place to live in, described in terms of heat, light, water and other environmental factors) and all the life that exists there. So **ecology** is the study of the interaction between the **environment** (the total sum of influences on an organism) and the organisms that are to be found there. Although the **biosphere**, the sum total of all ecosystems on Earth, is constantly changing as environmental factors change, there are long-term balances and checks that maintain stability.

Variation of environments and the living things that inhabit them is the key to a sustainable ecosystem. This variation allows minor imbalances in populations caused by random elements (such as pollution and disease) to be equalized. Through the rich diversity of life, a form of order is brought to the system – a fragile order is usually the result of one life form becoming too dominant, or too dependent on one primary producer.

Since the ecological **niches** (modes of life) of many different organisms overlap, as one life form declines another is able to step into the gap. If certain organisms dominated particular ecological niches, the whole ecosystem would depend on them. If, by some accident of genetics or pollution, they were to die out, the ecosystem would become seriously unbalanced.

Sustainable, balanced ecosystems develop gradually over very long periods of time. The introduction or extinction of a significant organism to a system will cause a significant realignment of its balance, which may take many years to correct and may seriously affect other organisms in that system. Such situations have arisen throughout recorded time – often as a result of the human importation of a foreign species which, in the absence of its natural predators, multiplies uncontrollably and causes havoc with the indigenous life.

Australia, the marsupial paradise, has suffered particularly badly in this respect. The introduction of the dingo from Asia about 3500 years ago spelt disaster for indigenous carnivores such as the thylacine, which now may only exist in Tasmania. The dromedary has found an excellent home in the outback, where the biggest wild herds in the world now exist. Cattle have thrived in Australia – but initially they led to the destruction of their own grazing lands: their dung would not decompose fast enough, killing the grass that it lay on and providing an excellent breeding ground for flies. The problem was solved with the introduction of the African dung beetle, which breaks up and buries the dung, reducing the ability of the flies to reproduce and also fertilizing the grassland. The rabbit, introduced to Australia as a food source, soon became a pest of plague proportions; its numbers were reduced by 'germ warfare' in the 1950s and 60s, in the form of a virus called myxomatosis.

The human influence has been to reduce diversity. Large-scale agriculture requires vast areas to be planted with the same species of plant so that efficient mechanical cropping is possible. This drastically reduces the variety of life that is able to exist in such areas – and those organisms that remain are usually regarded as pests and exterminated. Ecologies based on a small number of organisms (usually plants) are extremely susceptible to damage when environmental conditions are changed. The Amazonian basin has a poor level of nutrients in the soil, but the forest is able to thrive due to constant recycling through a wide range of different plants. Turning such land over to farming quickly exhausts the nutrients in the soil, causing crops to fail and desert conditions to develop unless a costly and constant programme of adding extra nutrients is followed. Inappropriate crops and too little crop variation has caused the Sahara Desert to expand greatly.

Types of relationship
Organisms can be connected within an ecosystem by a number of different types of relationship, including:
1. **Food relationships** – for example, between plant and consumer or between prey and predator (see Concept 2).
2. **Direct competition** – for example, between different animals that prey on the same species or that occupy the same habitat.
3. **Symbiosis** – a relationship of mutual benefit. An example of a symbiotic relationship is that between mammals and the bacteria that live in their intestines and help with the digestion of food.

The idea of 'biodiversity' and its implications are increasingly becoming important aspects of a child's general knowledge. Children frequently encounter 'awareness-raising' articles and TV programmes which may be frightening in both style and content. By increasing their level of understanding in this area, children will become better able to make informed decisions and to examine the issues effectively.

Why you need to know these facts

Vocabulary

Ecosystem – the sum total of an environment and the living things sharing it. The ways in which these living things interact determine the characteristics of the ecosystem.
Biosphere – the sum of all the ecosystems of the Earth.
Habitat – the particular environment in which an organism lives.
Environment – the conditions (both living and non-living) that surround an organism.
Symbiosis – interaction between two different species for mutual benefit.

Amazing facts

● There are between 10 and 100 million different species of living thing on Earth – by far the majority of which are microscopic.
● Approximately 50% of species on Earth in the year 2000 are predicted to be extinct by 2100.
● The tropical rainforests of South America, Africa, South-East Asia and Australia have the greatest variety of life: 50% of the Earth's species on 7% of its surface.

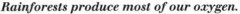

Common misconceptions

Rainforests produce most of our oxygen.
Well, it's a very good slogan for the 'Save the rainforest' groups, but it's quite wide of the mark. The **photoplankton** (photosynthesizing plankton) living in the ocean produce an estimated 90% of the oxygen released into the atmosphere. Land only accounts for about 28% of the Earth's surface, and of that only a small proportion is densely forested. All of the oceans, apart from the regions beneath the ice-caps, contain a layer of this plankton – providing a vast oxygen-producing surface area.

Questions

Why are there so many different species?
Long-term survival of a life form depends on variation: new species being just that little bit different to suffer less from a particular predator or disease, or to survive better in particular environmental conditions. By being slightly different from each other, or by living in slightly different places, a very wide variety of organisms can co-exist.

Why doesn't nature restore the balance in a damaged environment?
The simple answer is that it does. But it may take a long

time to restore the balance, and the new balance may be quite different from the old one. The balance possible in one kind of environment may be very different from the balance possible in another one: a valley that is flooded to provide a store of water will offer a very different environment for life from the one that existed there before. The 'balanced' environment that the Earth had 100 million years ago is very different from the one that exists today, and so the dominant life forms are very different. The environment is constantly changing, and all living things are constantly changing in response.

Why don't governments stop natural environments from being destroyed?

Humans are the dominant life form on this planet, and they tend to change their environment to suit their own short-term needs. Governments tend to be short-term in nature, so asking people to give up things such as cars or new homes in order to manage the long-term future of the environment is difficult for them to consider: they want to make people happy over the next five years, rather than the next fifty. In addition, vested commercial interests (such as major industries) have far more power to affect governments than 'the people'.

Teaching ideas

Habitat audit (observing, recording)

Take groups of children to different habitats around the school or beyond and attempt to identify the range of plants (and possibly minibeasts) living there.

Habitat comparisons (observing, recording)

Small groups can examine two different habitats (either by first-hand observation or using video and multimedia packages), and look for similarities and differences between them in terms of what organisms live there.

Environmental conditions (observing, inferring)

Small groups can find out what life forms are found in different environmental conditions (in terms of heat, light, water and so on), and attempt to describe the effects that the physical environment has on the variety of life found there. They could use direct observation of different environments such as the school pond and local park, or find out about environments such as 'the Arctic' and 'the desert'.

Micro-habitats (observing)

Sustainable ecosystems can be designed by introducing a range of compatible organisms to an enclosed environment. A school nature garden is often a good example of this: with a small amount of annual management, it can become almost self-sustaining. Usually some plants will need to be cut back to reduce their domination of the habitat; but otherwise, the garden will provide a home for a wide range of plants and small animals. Such areas provide excellent opportunities for long-term observation; an ongoing record can be kept on video (or photographs, taken on a seasonal basis) over a number of years, and used for comparison.

Concept 2: Food chains

Subject facts

All **biomass** – the organic mass of all living things on the planet – is derived (with a few exceptions) from energy produced by the Sun. There are a number of small organisms that gain their energy direct from volcanic vents in the ocean floor, and provide a food source for larger animals living there. However, most of the organisms that dwell in the depths of the ocean where sunlight never reaches are dependent on organisms from sunlit areas dying and sinking to provide food.

Primary producers

Apart from the limited exceptions described above, all life on this planet is dependent on **photosynthesis** (see Chapter 5, page 122). Without this process, life on Earth as we know it could not survive. Green plants and other green organisms (such as some forms of algae) use light energy to produce various forms of carbohydrate, which are then used as an energy source (food) by various animals, and by **decomposers** that survive on dead organic matter. These photosynthesizing organisms, such as grass, are known as **primary producers**.

The flow of energy

The organisms that live directly off the primary producers, such as rabbits, are called **herbivores,** or **first-order consumers**. These herbivores are often eaten by higher-order consumers or **carnivores**, such as foxes. Carnivores that hunt living food are known as **predators,** and their victims as **prey.** And so a **feeding chain** develops, linking higher-order consumers to primary producers.

Often a **pyramid** of biomass can be used to represent these feeding relationships. For example, consider the simple chain of grass–rabbit–fox. It will require a large mass of grass to sustain sufficient numbers of rabbits to feed one fox for a given period of time. Not all of the energy obtained by the grass from the sunlight will be passed onto these rabbits: they can't eat all of the grass. Also, much of the energy consumed by a rabbit will be used for movement and to keep the rabbit warm, and so will not be available to the fox when it feeds on the rabbit. In this way, energy is 'lost' from the living system at each level of the pyramid.

The pyramid of biomass is also a pyramid of numbers of different species. In most cases, a first-order consumer can rely on a wide range of primary producers to satisfy its food requirements. Likewise, most higher-level consumers have a range of food sources that they can utilize – humans, for example, can eat a range of both primary producers and lower-level consumers. But the higher up the pyramid you go, the more limited your range of food sources is likely to be, and so the number of niches available in the ecosystem is smaller. It's tough at the top!

Energy dependency

If a species of consumer is wholly dependent on a particular food source, it is in a precarious position. Any loss of that food source will lead to its immediate extinction. By being able to rely on a range of foods, the species can move on to other food sources as they become available (perhaps on a seasonal basis). The numbers of particular animals will vary according to their food supply.

For example, if environmental conditions allow a large number of aphids to survive over the winter, there will be an abundance of them the following year – which will allow their main predator, the ladybird, to increase rapidly in numbers. This increase in the number of predators will reduce the aphid numbers, causing the ladybird to starve through lack of adequate food supplies until a lower balance is once more restored. This is an example of how the feeding relationships between organisms in an environment can preserve a balance over a period of time.

Decomposers

Dead organic material also provides a starting point for an energy chain. The energy content of a dead plant or animal can be utilized by **decomposers** (a general term for life forms that use only dead organisms as an energy source). This can happen at a higher, **scavenging** level (as in the carrion crow) or at a lower, **detrivore** level (as in fungi). Decomposers that break down detritus such as leaf litter and small dead animals return nutrients to the soil. They may also be themselves a source of food for animals.

Why you need to know these facts

The flow of energy from the sun to animals (such as us) is a complex process, but is one that children need to develop an understanding of in order to appreciate how living things are connected to each other.

Vocabulary

Biomass – the total organic mass of living things in an ecosystem.
Primary producers – organisms (such as green plants) that use sunlight as their energy source.
Herbivores – animals that eat plants.
Carnivores – animals that eat other animals.
Decomposers – living things (animals or fungi) that do not feed on other living things, but use dead organic matter as their food source.

Amazing facts

Food chains are seldom more than four links long: vegetation, herbivore, small carnivore, large carnivore. You will not find cat steaks or bear chops at your local butcher's. Large carnivores are quite edible – but there aren't so many of them, and they're not so easy to catch!

Common misconceptions

All species live together in harmony/try to kill and eat each other/compete with each other.
Be very wary of statements which begin 'All species...' All three of these statements are true for a range of organisms – but not for all species. Anyone would be hard-pressed to find a convincing argument about how haddock and rabbits are out to destroy, or even compete with, each other! Animals within a given ecosystem may compete, have a predator-prey relationship or even exist in symbiosis (see page 153) – or they may occupy niches that prevent their having any direct relationship.

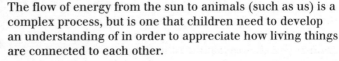

Scavengers are lower forms of life.
This belief might come from the feeling that finding and
consuming living things that have already died is not quite
'right' and is 'dirty'. Scavengers such as crows, vultures or
hyenas are perhaps not the cutest of animals, but they are
certainly not lower life forms in scientific terms. Even in
terms of their roles, they perform an indispensable service,
ensuring that once-living things are reduced to their base
chemical forms as quickly as possible so that they can be
recycled. Perhaps they should be held in higher regard in
these days of ecological awareness!

Human beings are natural carnivores/herbivores.
One of the key factors that have made humans the dominant
life form on this planet is their versatility. They are quite
capable of feeding on either animals or plants – but a
balanced mixture of both seems to work best.

Questions

*If green plants need their own food, why do some eat
insects?*
Carnivorous plants such as the Venus fly-trap usually live in
areas where there are insufficient nutrients in the soil. They
have adapted to these conditions by attracting, trapping and
then digesting insects for the nutrients that they contain
(mainly nitrogen). Clearly these plants, like those that
attract insects using flowers, evolved and developed long
after animals had appeared on Earth.

*If we are carnivores/herbivores, why can't we eat raw
meat/raw vegetables?*
The simple answer is that we can – and for much of our
history, we probably did! The act of cooking makes certain
types of food easier to digest, and destroys many of the
harmful microbes that raw food can contain. In vegetables,
this usually results in the long and complex molecules and
fibres being broken into smaller chains that the enzymes in
our digestive tract can digest more readily. Cooking meat
allows tougher pieces to be eaten, as slow heating
tenderizes the meat fibres. Make sure the children are
aware that eating raw meat or fish may be very dangerous,
as the food may be infected with bacteria.

Food chains (researching, recording, presenting)

Teaching ideas

Small groups or individuals can research a higher-order
consumer (such as the fox, lion or orca) using appropriate

sources (books, the Internet, multimedia CD-ROMs and so on) to identify their foods. They can then identify the 'foods of the foods', working down through the food chain until they reach a primary producer. The food chains could then be presented as posters.

Food webs (identifying, presenting)

Provide enough information cards for each child in the class to assume the role of an organism within a small ecosystem (such as a pond, field or savannah). Each card should have the name of the organism, where it gets its food energy (sunlight or other organisms) and what eats it. Armed with these cards, the children must find the other organisms that they are linked to. The links can be formalized with lengths of coloured wool, held tight between the members of the food web. If one element within the web is made extinct, the effects can clearly be seen by the way the web unravels. Figure 1 shows an example of a food web diagram.

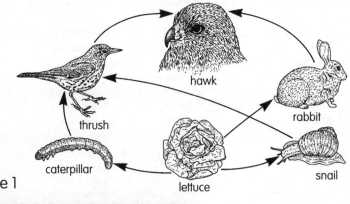

hawk

thrush

rabbit

caterpillar

lettuce

snail

Figure 1

Concept 3: Adaptation to environment

Fitting into the pattern

Many animals are 'designed' to fill equivalent niches within different ecosystems. Herring are well adapted to browsing on surface plankton, rather as rabbits are adapted to browsing on grassland – but if you were to swap them over, neither would be particularly impressed. Both have evolved to a point where their design allows them to live in particular environmental conditions: they could not survive in each other's habitat.

Often, it is quite surprising how well species **do** adapt to new or changed environments. Mice have been known to adapt to living in refrigerated food stores by growing thicker coats; the fox has turned from hunter to scavenger in urban areas; pigeons are so common in most cities that they have become pests. With a modicum of background knowledge, it is possible to deduce a considerable amount about the environment that an animal inhabits by observing the animal. Fins imply an aquatic lifestyle; thick fur or blubber implies a cold habitat. The animals that inhabit a particular environment will tend to have similar characteristics.

Adapted for a purpose

Some key adaptations in animals relate to their sources of food and eating habits. If we just stick to vertebrates (it simplifies matters no end), then a closer inspection of the jaw and the teeth can provide a lot of useful information. Different types of teeth (or beak – see Chapter 2, page 33) perform different tasks. From looking at the size and prominence of the teeth, deductions can be made about diet (see Figure 2):

● Lots of big canines – carnivore. The jaw will probably only be able to move up and down, gripping and tearing. The shark is a particularly impressive example.

● No canines, lots of well-developed molars – herbivore. The jaw will move from side to side, grinding. The horse has incisors to cut vegetation and molars to grind it up.

● A mixture of canines and molars – omnivore. Human teeth provide an obvious example of this design.

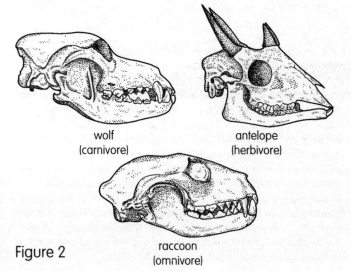

wolf
(carnivore)

antelope
(herbivore)

raccoon
(omnivore)

Figure 2

By observing the limbs (if any), judgements can be made about the animal's means of locomotion and how swift it may be in relation to its size. All study of this kind is about looking for clues that can be linked to prior knowledge. Many animals will be familiar to children, but too little is remembered about why they are found in that habitat. Ignorance of this aspect of animal life is one reason why many 'famous' animals (such as the tiger) are being allowed to die out as their environments are destroyed.

In looking at classification (see Chapter 6, page 137), we saw that it is less important to know the name of an animal than to know how to find it by using sorting keys and relating it to other animals. Understanding an animal's way of life works in a similar way. Yes, the lion hunts, kills and eats other animals – but why does it do that? What features of a lion make that possible? Where does it live?

Local habitats

There are usually places near the school that offer a range of different habitats, such as a pond, tree, bush or area of leaf litter (see Teaching ideas below). These all have their own particular inhabitants, adapted to living in that location. Close examination of minibeasts in their natural habitat will provide good indications of how they are adapted for those particular environmental conditions. Their eating habits are often less easy to determine: the discovery of a particular minibeast on a particular plant may mean that it eats that plant, or that it hunts another minibeast that lives on the plant, or that it lays eggs on the plant so that its young can eat it.

Plant adaptations

Like animals, plants are adapted for living in different habitats. Some plants are tolerant of salt water, others are not; some need copious amounts of water, other can survive on mist; some can survive freezing temperatures, other can survive dry heat. Even locally, it is possible to see how plants adapt through changes in their growth. In long grass, dandelions will grow tall; on lawns, they will flatten themselves and spread out horizontally.

Why you need to know these facts

When observing animals, plants and other living things, an important aspect to consider is how they fit in with their environment: how they are adapted to the particular niche that they fill. This will help to explain a lot about an organism's structure, behaviour and habitat.

Niche – the position of a particular species within a food web in a given environment.
Adaptation – the ways in which an organism is particularly suited to its environment.

Vocabulary

● Cacti take in carbon dioxide at night and store it to use in photosynthesis during the day. Opening the stomata during the day to take in carbon dioxide would result in the loss of moisture, which they cannot afford to do in dry, desert conditions.
● Penguins have down on the tops of their feet to rest their eggs on, because the ground is too cold for the egg to sit on.

Amazing facts

Giraffes live in the jungle.
There is still a widespread misconception that Africa is mostly jungle. Also, this is an indication of a general misconception about the nature of a jungle. Humans, let alone larger animals, would have difficulty in moving around in densely forested areas. Get the children to think it through for themselves! Yes, the animal is able to reach the leaves at the tops of trees; but if the trees were very close together, how would it be able to move through them? If you wanted to eat the leaves at the tops of trees and they were close together, why go down to the ground? Why not just move directly from tree to tree, like a gibbon? Clearly, the trees must be further apart and generally not too tall for the giraffe's shape to be a successful adaptation.

Common misconceptions

Each animal is perfectly adapted or ideally suited to its environment.
The environments that organisms live in are dynamic places, constantly changing – and so are the organisms that live there. When considering the adaptation of an animal to its environment, we have to think about all the other animals living there and the relationships between them. A species will survive if it is able to exploit a particular niche better than any other. If another animal, better adapted for that particular niche, comes along, the original species will have to adapt – or else face possible extinction. It has always been the case that species have developed over time before dying out.

How do animals become adapted to their environment?
See the notes on variation above. Evolutionary change is by
no means a sudden process, in which one minute you are
flapping your arms madly, and the next you are soaring
through the sky. With each new generation, there are small
changes due to the inexact transfer of genetic information.
Most of these changes are of no consequence. Some
changes make it harder for the animal to survive, so it will
be less likely to breed and pass on the new traits. Some
changes make the animal more successful (for example, as
a food gatherer), increasing its chances of breeding and
thus passing on those traits to future generations.

Overall, adaptation is a matter of chance: sometimes the
changes link into the environment, sometimes they don't.
The ones that do are usually the ones that continue and
develop further.

***Why don't our bodies adapt to changes in the
environment?***
Actually, they do. The immediate changes are often simple
small ones: we shiver when we are cold and sweat when we
are hot. The bigger changes take much more time to
achieve. Before humans were able to change their
environments (through such devices as air conditioning and
central heating), different races evolved to exploit different
environments. The Inuit (Eskimo) people evolved to survive
in the extreme cold of Arctic conditions, while the people of
the Amazon basin became physically adapted to the hot and
humid conditions there. Adaptation on a significant scale
takes a long time – these days, we are more likely to change
our environment to suit us than to evolve to suit our
environment.

***Why don't animals adapt to kill all the animals that
they compete with?***
They are probably trying to. But at the same time that they
are doing this, the animals that they are competing with are
also adapting to fight back or run faster!

Design a beastie (observing, inferring)
The children, working in pairs or in small groups, can look
at a particular habitat (such as a pond, forest, desert or back
garden). They can start by researching its inhabitants and
the roles that they have in the ecology. Their task is to
design a new beastie to fit in with that environment. They

should draw the animal and describe what it eats, what eats it, its habits, its mobility and any other aspects that they feel to be important.

Habitat hunt (observing, inferring)
Give small groups of children a description and/or pictures of an animal that they are not likely to be familiar with. From the information provided, they have to say as much as they can about the animal: what it eats, where it lives and so on, giving reasons for their suggestions. They can go on to find out how accurate they were by researching in books or multimedia encyclopaedias.

Local habitats (observing, recording)
Groups of children can visit different local environments (such as a pond, hedge or patch of waste ground), closely observe the animals living there and note how each is adapted for life in that particular habitat.

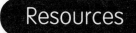

Resources

For a list of minibeast collection and observation equipment, see Chapter 6, page 149.

Reference material
Provide photographs and posters of different habitats. Star *Science Reception Resource Book* provides some imaginative examples of 'home corners' turned into habitats: underwater, arctic, rainforest and so on. The following are good starting points for Internet searches:
- *www.ase.org.uk*
- *www.nhm.org.uk*
- *www.mnh.si.edu*

General CD-ROM encyclopaedias such as *Britannica* and *Microsoft Encarta* provide an excellent range of multimedia information. The *Eyewitness* series from DK Multimedia are also useful sources.

Life processes
GLOSSARY

WHAT IS LIFE?

Alive or **living** – displays all of the characteristics of a living thing (growth, energy use, reproduction).

Animals – multicellular organisms that co-ordinate movement through nerve impulses.

Dormant – has the potential for life when the environmental conditions are suitable.

Ectotherm – an animal with no internal control of its body temperature.

Endotherm – an animal with internal control of its body temperature.

Kingdom – the major classification of different groups of living organisms.

Never alive – contains no material that was once alive (unless that material has since changed significantly in chemical structure and composition).

Phylum – the first step down in classification from a kingdom. A phylum gathers together organisms that share major structural features.

Plants – multicellular photosynthesizing organisms.

Prokaryotes – micro-organisms (including **bacteria**) that lack a cell nucleus.

Species – a group of living things that are so closely related that viable interbreeding is possible.

VERTEBRATES

Adult – the final stage of the life cycle, in which reproduction is possible.

Beak – an elongated appendage around a bird's mouth,

made from a material similar to human fingernails.

Bill – a name given to a beak of the flatter (duck-like) type or the smaller (pigeon-like) type.

Froglet – the stage of development of a frog which exhibits characteristics of both the tadpole and the mature frog.

Gill – a set of thin membranes that absorb oxygen out of water, allowing fish and other aquatic animals to 'breathe' underwater.

Larva – an immature stage of the life cycle.

Marsupial – a mammal that carries its young in a pouch, where it feeds and completes its development.

Metamorphosis – a fundamental change in the body shape and lifestyle of an animal.

Monotreme – an egg-laying mammal.

Tadpole – the larval, aquatic stage of a frog's development.

Talons – the grasping claws of a bird of prey.

Web – skin between toes to aid swimming.

MAMMALS

Adolescent – an immature adult stage in which reproductive capability and other adult characteristics are developing.

Adult – the stage of development in which the individual is fully capable of reproduction.

Aerobic respiration – the release of energy in body tissues, using oxygen.

Anaerobic respiration – the short-term release of energy without the use of oxygen, leading to a build-up of lactic acid.

Antagonistic pair – two muscles which are attached to bones in such a way that they can cause a movement and the reverse of that movement.

Arteries – the tubes carrying blood away from the heart.

Atria (plural of **atrium**) – the smaller heart chambers through which the blood passes to reach the ventricles.

Brain – the organ that receives and analyzes sensory input, and controls actions.

Canines – ripping teeth.

Capillaries – very fine (small-bore) blood vessels.

Cartilage – a flexible, hard-wearing material that protects bones from damage within joints.

Cochlea – the sound-sensitive part of the inner ear.

Semicircular canals – the part of the inner ear that maintains balance by registering changes in position.

Colon – the large intestine, where the undigested food has moisture removed from it and dead red blood cells are added prior to excretion.

Cones – the colour-sensitive cells in the retina, only responsive to bright light.

Cornea – the tough outer covering of the eye.

Diaphragm – a muscle sheet that allows air to be drawn into the lungs.

Digestion – the process of breaking food down into simple chemicals for absorption by the body.

Duodenum – the upper part of the small intestine, where further enzymes and bile are added to the chyme to break down the more complex foods.

Echolocation – the use of echoed sounds to 'see' objects in the dark.

Heart – the muscle that pumps the blood around the body.

Ileum – the lower end of the small intestine where the digested food is absorbed into the body via the blood supply.

Incisors – cutting teeth.

Infant – the stage of development immediately following birth, when there is still a high dependence on the mother or family group for nourishment.

Involuntary – nervous messages that are sent automatically (for example, to control the heartbeat).

Iris – the coloured outer ring of the pupil that regulates the amount of light entering the eye.

Ligament – tissue that connects bones together and surrounds joints.

Lungs – the organs that extract oxygen from the air.

Molars – grinding teeth.

Mouth – where food is physically broken down into smaller pieces and moisture is added.

Muscle – fibrous tissue capable of contracting and combining glucose with oxygen to release energy.

Optic lens – the part of the eye that focuses light onto the retina.

Pinna – the outer portion of the ear.

Pulse – the rhythmic flow of blood along the arteries.

Pupil – the black centre of the eye that allows light through to the lens.

Red blood cells – cells that carry oxygen and carbon dioxide in the bloodstream.

Reflex – an involuntary reaction in response to a particular stimulus.

Retina – the light-sensitive inner coating of the eyeball.

Rods – retinal cells that are sensitive to motion, but not to colour.

Saliva – a lubricating digestive juice produced in the mouth.

Spinal cord – a long nerve that is the main conduit for messages and signals to and from the brain.

Stomach – a rounded vessel in the body where acidic digestive juices are added to the food to reduce it to a 'thick soup' called chyme.

Taste buds – the taste-sensitive cells on the tongue and at the back of the mouth.

Tendon – very strong, inelastic tissue that connects muscles to bones.

Valves – flaps of muscle that are positioned to prevent the reverse flow of blood.

Veins – the tubes carrying blood towards the heart.

Ventricles – the large, muscular chambers of the heart.

Voluntary – nervous messages involving conscious actions such as walking.

HUMANS

Addiction – a physical craving for a substance, which can lead to 'withdrawal symptoms'.

Carbohydrates (such as starches and sugars) – foods used by the body to make energy.

Cholesterol – a fatty substance that preserves nerve fibres.

Drug – any chemical that enters and has an effect on the body.

Embryo – the early stage of development of the fertilized ovum.

Foetus – the later, distinctively human phase of development of the embryo leading up to birth.

Fats – energy-rich foods which represent special energy stores in an animal or plant.

Fibre – indigestible material that aids the movement of food along the digestive tract.

Immunization (or **vaccination**) – the act of injecting a vaccine in order to provoke the body to develop antibodies against particular infections.

Malnutrition – the effects of a poorly balanced diet.

Minerals (such as iron and calcium) – trace elements in foods, used in the manufacture of certain body parts (for example, blood and bones).

Non-prescription medicines – ones which can be bought from chemists and administered by a responsible adult.

Nutrition – the way in which we (and other living things) gain energy from food.

Ovum – the egg; the female contribution to reproduction.

Peristalsis – muscular action to move food along the digestive tubes.

Placenta – a growth within the uterus that provides the foetus with its blood supply.

Prescription medicines – ones which are prescribed for a particular person with a particular illness, and should not be taken by anyone else.

Protein (such as meat and cheese) – foods used by the body to manufacture and repair cells.

Sexual reproduction – the combining of genetic material from two individuals to produce a new life.

Sperm – a mobile cell which contains the male contribution to reproduction.

Starvation – the effects of a prolonged lack of food.

Tobacco – a highly addictive, carcinogenic substance made from the leaves of the tobacco plant, and containing the drug nicotine.

Uterus – a special organ in the female abdomen which provides an environment for the developing embryo and foetus.

Vitamins – chemicals in foods that are essential (in small quantities) for the physical well-being of the body.

Water – the fluid in which all of the above, after digestion, are dissolved in order to be absorbed by the body.

PLANTS

Bulb – a swollen, layered stem base from which regrowth is possible.

Chlorophyll – the chemical that makes the photosynthesis process work.

Catalyst – a substance that enables a chemical reaction to take place.

Cone – a woody 'fruit' with scales that protect the seeds.

Conifer – a cone-bearing tree or shrub.

Dormant – when growth is suspended at a very low level of metabolism.

Fertilization – the point at which the sperm from the pollen meets the egg in the ovary.

Germination – the point at which the dormant embryo begins to grow into a seedling.

Ovule – the part of the ovary that contains the egg.

Photosynthesis – the process by which light energy is used to convert carbon dioxide and water in to glucose and oxygen.

Pistil – the female part of the flower, containing the **stigma**, **style** and **ovary**.

Pollen – the granule that delivers the male genetic material to the female seed.

Pollination – the process by which the pollen reaches the stigma.

Stamen – the male part of the flower, comprising the **anther** and **filament**.

Transpiration – water loss from plant leaves, causing more water to be drawn up through the roots.
Tuber – a swollen root from which regrowth is possible.

Body segments – the number of clearly defined sections a minibeast has, including the head and/or tail. An insect has three body segments, an arachnid two.
Key – a questioning device that allows the progressive narrowing down of the classification of an unknown living thing (or object) based on its observable or testable features.
Larva – an immature form which bears little resemblance to the adult form.
Metamorphosis – a process of change from one form to another during a life cycle.
Minibeast – common term for a small invertebrate.
Nymph – an immature form that bears some resemblance to the adult (the differences are usually that the adult form has wings and reproductive organs, and has a different habitat and food source).
Pooter – a device for sucking smaller minibeasts into a specimen container.

ENVIRONMENT

Adaptation – the ways in which an organism is particularly suited to its environment.
Biomass – the total mass of living things in an ecosystem.
Biosphere – the sum of all the ecosystems of the Earth.
Carnivores – animals that eat other animals.
Decomposers – living things (animals or fungi) that do not feed on other living things, but use dead organic matter as their food source.
Ecosystem – the sum total of an environment and the living things sharing it. The ways in which these living things interact determine the characteristics of the ecosystem.
Environment – the conditions (both living and non-living) that surround an organism.
Habitat – the particular environment in which an organism lives.
Herbivores – animals that eat plants.
Niche – the position of a particular species within a food web in a given environment.
Primary producers – organisms (such as green plants) that use sunlight as their energy source.
Symbiosis – interaction between two different species for mutual benefit.

Life processes

INDEX